SELLING YOUR
BUSINESS

SELLING YOUR BUSINESS

Begin with the
End in Mind

DAVID A. KING

BUSINESS EXIT EDUCATION

King, David.

Selling your business—begin with the end in mind

Copyright © 2020 by Business Exit Education

Library of Congress Control Number:2019917240

ISBN: 978-1-7342047-0-4

ISBN: 978-1-7342047-1-1

This publication is designed to provide accurate and authoritative
information regarding the subject matter covered. It is sold with the
understanding that neither the publisher nor the author is rendering legal
or other professional services. If legal advice or other expert assistance
is required, the services of a competent, licensed professional should be
sought.

If you wish to purchase multiple copies, please contact the author
David King at david@biz-exit.com.

TABLE OF CONTENTS

Contents

Dedication

This book is dedicated to all my past and present clients who have given me the privilege of representing their businesses. Whether a major Wall Street Investment Bank, a Silicon Valley high-tech company, or a mom and pop service business, each client has been an education for me, giving me the experience necessary to write this book.

This book is also dedicated to my grandfather, Jackson "Pappy" King, who built a successful small business in the Florida citrus industry. His children succeeded him and ultimately sold the business 53 years after it opened.

Acknowledgments

Special thanks to colleagues, friends and family whose contributions made this book complete. I was lucky to be born into a business-minded family, including Joe King, Jack King, Michael King, and Sandra King. Without our mother and family Chief Financial Officer, Blair King, none of us could balance our books.

Thanks to Kirk Michie, a wealth advisor with AB Bernstein, and Martin Staubus, an Employee Stock Ownership Plan consultant with the Beyster Institute at UC San Diego. Special thanks to Tim Malott and Thor Eakes for their input and reviews.

SELLING YOUR BUSINESS

Introduction:

Small and middle-market businesses are the engine of the U.S. economy. According to the U.S. Census, there are 5.9 million firms and 6.4 million establishments that employ fewer than 500 employees in the United States. These 12.4 million businesses account for 90.2 percent of all the businesses in the United States.

The U.S. Small Business Administration ("SBA") reports that there are 29.6 million small businesses employing 57.9 employees (47.8%) of the total U.S. employees. The SBA defines a "small business" as one that employs 1 to 1,500 employees, depending on industry category. However, many consider small businesses as those with fewer than 100 employees and mid-sized businesses to have between 100 and 999 employees. Small businesses are also referred to as "Main Street businesses".

Depending upon the geographic location and industry of a business, a middle-market company may be one with revenue ranging from $5 million or $10 million up to $500 million or $1 billion.

According to data from BizBuySell.com, a record number of businesses were sold in the U.S. in 2018. The table below shows the number of small business transactions and annual growth rate over a four-year period.

Year	Transactions	Increase Over Prior Year
2015	7,222	
2016	7,842	8.6%
2017	9,919	26.5%
2018	10,312	4.0%

This book is written for all owners of small to middle-market businesses who are planning to exit from their businesses and trusted members of management. Business owners may "exit" their business in a variety of ways described herein, but this book is focused on sales to independent, third-party buyers.

Selling a business is the American dream – the pot of gold at the end of the rainbow, the reward for years of hard work. Entrepreneurs need not neglect the rest of their lives to build a successful business, but they often do. Most successful business owners have made countless sacrifices in hopes that they would someday reap the benefits of their labor and live a new life of vacations, recreation, comfort, and prosperity.

Deciding to miss the ball game, the play, the concert, because you've resolved to work and invest in your family's future. And taking responsibility for the consequences of those actions. Patience. Frugality. Sacrifice.

When you boil it down, what do those three things have in common? Those are choices. Money is not peace of mind. Money's not happiness. Money is, at its essence that measure of [one's] choices.[1]

This book will help business owners prepare for this major milestone and close a successful sale.

This book will set forth the business sale process and provide useful information to guide a seller's decision-making, before and during the sale process. This book is about the sale of privately-owned businesses, not publicly traded ones.

As an entrepreneur of a privately-owned company, you have several alternatives on how to exit your business:

- Continue working at your business until your disability or death,
- Reduce your time commitment to the business substantially and let someone else operate the business until your full retirement or death,
- Liquidate the business, voluntarily or involuntarily,
- Successfully sell the business to an independent buyer, or
- Consummate an internal succession to management, your partners, or your family.

You must take control of your "exit plan" to make it a positive one:

In the absence of a valid exit strategy, events will inexorably dictate the final exit plan for the business. Exit plans may be as varied as each venture's needs and purposes. In the absence of an Exit Plan, it is probable that an involuntary exit will be enforced by any number of circumstances: loss of market, competition, a better mouse trap, changes in customer acceptance, inept management, catering to wants instead of needs, lack of cost controls, etc.[2]

The purpose of this book is to avoid an "involuntary exit" and achieve success through the exit strategy of your choosing. An involuntary exit may be caused by death, disability, divorce, disagreement or distress.

Selling a business requires a team of professionals. These services can be expensive. Advance preparation will help an owner receive the full benefit of these services and keep the process moving smoothly in order to mitigate these fees.

Selling a business is a job in and of itself. Managing and selling a business is like working two or even three jobs. This is the final mile of a marathon which seems to last ten miles.

You must continue to operate your business as if no sale were imminent. Acquisitions fall through more often than not. You may own your company longer than you anticipated after you have made the decision to sell. Thus, you need to keep your business operating as profitably as possible. From beginning to end, the sale process may take years.

Timing is crucial. Many young entrepreneurs try to sell their businesses too early, and seasoned business owners start the process too late.

You may believe you should not sell your business because it is generating plenty of cash. This is usually the right time to sell your business. This book not only stresses the need to start planning immediately, but it also guides you to choose the right time to exit your business.

Read this book more than once. Read it over a long weekend. Read it again before you begin the sale process. Scrub each individual chapter by itself and take notes when beginning each component of the sale process. I touch upon most of the major deal terms and concepts in multiple chapters. Don't worry if a topic is difficult on your first pass. It's coming again later.

Several factors impacting your exit are outside your control, but you need a greater awareness of them and a better ability to gauge these factors. However, in the short-term, there are important considerations under your control that require special focus and heightened attention, such as:

- Increasing the value and acquisition appeal of your business
- Improving operating efficiencies, productivity, and accounting
- Working with a team of competent and experienced business professionals to develop an exit plan
- Implementing a detailed and strategic process to sell your business.

You should be aware of all the key factors within your control and keep them in your mindful grasp. Reading this book should make you better prepared to deal with every aspect of the sale of your business and impress upon you the need to start planning immediately.

Two Entrepreneurs and Their Businesses

Through the chapters of this book I will share the story of two businesses and their owners. You will see how their choices impact their business development and each stage of the sales process.

Zack, Southern Electrical Supplies, Inc.

Zack founded Southern Electrical Supplies, Inc. ("SES") in 1991. SES is a wholesaler of electrical supplies, selling in Florida, Georgia and Alabama. SES has revenue of over $10 million per year, which is growing steadily at approximately seven percent per year. SES sells to a broad range of retailers, electricians and general contractors with a niche in sales for state, federal and local government construction projects.

Zack worked in construction as a teenager and through college. He majored in building construction from Southern State University. After obtaining his bachelor's degree, his career transitioned from construction into sales of electrical components working for AVX Corporation. After obtaining his MBA at night school from Atlanta Occidental College, he was promoted to Vice President of Sales where he worked for another eight years.

Zack saved a modest sum while working for AVX, mostly in his 401(k) account. He purchased and remodeled a home which was his most valuable asset.

Before he quit AVX, Zack spoke with a mentor at the local Small Business Administration office and with his uncle who recently sold his construction framing business. SES had three employees at its inception and now has a total of 35 employees split among sales, warehouse, and logistics, as well as administrative management.

HARRY, ELEGANT CATERING, LLC

Harry and his former business partner, Skip, founded Elegant Catering, LLC in 2012. Harry and Skip were childhood friends. Elegant Catering operates in Dana Point, California. The business has generated as much as $4 million in annual revenue, but only $2.5 million last year.

Harry worked at several restaurants through high school and college. He attended Pacific State University where he majored in political science and was active in his fraternity. After graduating from college, Harry worked as a mortgage broker and was a bartender at a popular restaurant in Newport Beach.

Harry's mortgage brokerage business declined in 2007. He predicted the imminent crash in real estate, so he enrolled at Downtown Law School. After law school, Harry opened a solo practice where he handled DUI and personal injury cases. Although the practice of law generated a few lucrative months, Harry did not enjoy the required attention to detail and the grind of working as an attorney.

Skip worked in restaurants, real estate and property management since high school. After high school, Skip took a full-time job at Bayside Views, a high-end property where he managed events and banquets. With Skip's extensive relationships at Bayside Views, the partners were able to corner the market on catering at the property when they founded Elegant Catering.

Chapter One:

START PLANNING TO SELL YOUR BUSINESS ON DAY ONE

Entrepreneurs should learn this valuable lesson: to effectively prepare for the sale of your business you should begin planning on day one. Mistakes at the founding of a business can have expensive consequences when it comes time to exit the business. The longer you wait to plan for your sale, the fewer alternatives you may have for structuring your exit.

THE BUSINESS ENTITY AND TAXES

When forming a legal business entity, owners should consider the tax implications of the ultimate sale. Generally, a business can be organized as a sole proprietorship, partnership, limited liability company ("LLC"), or a corporation. A corporation may be taxed as a "C corporation" which is subject to federal income taxes or as an "S corporation" which is a "flow-through" entity, meaning that income is not taxed at the corporate level, but "flows through" to the owners who are taxed on their share of net income.

Most buyers of a business will prefer to structure the transaction as an asset acquisition as opposed to buying the stock of your company. In fact, your buyer is unlikely to purchase the stock of your corporation. Purchasing stock may not allow the buyer to step-up the tax basis in the assets of your business, and thus a stock sale would reduce the buyer's tax benefits following the sale.

If an entity is organized as a C corporation, the taxes owed following an asset sale may be nearly double the tax liability if the entity had been organized as an S corporation. Even businesses that are sold in multiple transactions benefit from maintaining "flow-through" tax treatment. Private equity investors may use flow-through business entities (i.e. those which are not taxed separately at the corporate level).

The gain or income which flows through to the owners of an S corporation is taxed once for income tax purposes at the owner's rates (depending upon the character of the assets being sold). Qualified Small Businesses are C corporations that may be used to minimize or defer a taxable event. If your business conducts a "qualified business" (such as technology, retail, wholesale, and manufacturing) and its assets do not exceed $50 million, your stock may obtain Qualified Small Business Stock (QSBS) treatment and avoid a portion of the gain upon sale.

Business owners should understand the tax attributes of their company years in advance of a sale. On the eve of a sale, it will be too late to make most changes. A lack of tax planning could wind up costing business owners millions in extra taxes, raining on the parade of the closing day. As you can see, consultation with a tax advisor/accountant is essential — prior to founding a business.

Intellectual Property Protection

Someone selling a hardware store would not expect to receive the full price for their business if they didn't keep locks and alarms on the doors and maintain good records of the inventory. Similarly, companies should protect and keep good records of all their valuable assets including their intangible assets and intellectual property.

On day one, a company should develop an intellectual property protection strategy identifying all of its intellectual property (or "IP") and how the IP should be registered and protected. Should the company register a trademark, file a patent application, seek enhanced copyright protection of everything reduced to writing, or should the company maintain trade secrets?

Certain intangible assets, such as customer lists, may not fall into the traditional definition of intellectual property. However, this proprietary information should be protected from disclosure, and employees should contractually agree to treat all proprietary information as trade secrets.

An effectively managed company not only identifies and registers its valuable intellectual property. It also protects its intellectual property in contracts executed with its employees, contractors, and vendors. A well-organized business executes proper licensing agreements when it uses another company's intellectual property or allows another business to use its own intellectual property. It is not difficult to keep all these crucial records organized for periodic reviews and updates, the lack of which may indicate the absence of diligent intellectual property protection.

CAPITALIZATION

The stock and other equity ownership of the company (which along with debt are the "capitalization" of a business) should be properly managed by its board of directors with proper legal advice from corporate counsel. All too often, corporations hand out stock to new employees like Monopoly money, without considering proper board authorization, tax implications, or the valuation of the stock transferred to the employee. A sloppily drafted employment offer letter to a long-forgotten former member of management can put a company in a bind when trying to close a sale.

Whenever issuing stock — to anyone — contact your corporate counsel. With stock issued to employees, keep in mind this should be an opportunity for a valuable member of the team to take an ownership stake in the company, not to mess up the company's capitalization.

A corporation must have accurate records of its stock ownership, reflecting properly authorized and executed share transactions, in order to preserve any possibility of selling the company through a stock sale. A stock sale is usually a more tax-efficient way to sell a company and a cleaner way to close a long chapter of the owners' involvement in the business.

ACCOUNTING

A company should maintain the accounting staff appropriate for a business of its size and sophistication. A business owner will pay a dear price for skimping on accounting staff and service providers — both its internal and external accountants.

All too often, boot-strapping entrepreneurs remain one step behind in the level of accounting information system they maintain, including the qualifications and management level of its top financial officer. This is penny-wise and pound-foolish, and it can reduce the purchase price or even kill a deal when a buyer scrubs the books prior to closing.

How do you determine the appropriate size of your accounting staff and sophistication of your accounting information system? Ask your CPA or ask several CPAs. If your own CPA cannot provide helpful guidance on how to build an accounting system suited for a business of your size and industry, he or she may not be the best qualified CPA to support you through the long-term development of your business.

FreshBooks, QuickBooks, and Sage 50 cloud are common entry-level accounting software, but numerous other alternatives are available. Depending upon the number of transaction processing functions which will interface directly with your general ledger (such as accounts payable, accounts receivable, inventory, payroll, and fixed assets) and the volume and aggregate dollar amount of transactions you process, your business should eventually graduate from entry-level software to a more sophisticated accounting system which your IT and accounting professionals will implement and manage.

AVOID OR ELIMINATE DEAL KILLERS

Your business operations may generate deal killers: litigation, tax liabilities (particularly employment-related taxes), environmental liabilities, unreasonable product liabilities, and other risks too big for a buyer to assume. If the buyer will operate the same business under the same name, the buyer will get dragged into any impending litigation whether they assume such liabilities or not.

Be careful when entering any significant agreement. Look for the "assignment clause" in every contract you sign and try to avoid such clauses which require your counterparty's consent (their permission) in order to assign the contract (i.e., transfer the contract to your buyer). This can delay or frustrate your sale.

If your company is not organized as a flow-through entity for tax purposes, the tax burden may be problematic and even fatal. Ideally the buyer could purchase your stock, but buyers are reluctant to take upon the risk of unknown liabilities and prefer the tax treatment of an asset sale. If the buyer would agree to a stock sale, they are likely to discount the price and structure the deal to provide extra protection from future liabilities.

INCENTIVIZE KEY EMPLOYEES TO SUPPORT A SALE

You can incentivize key employees to promote your business development and future sale. These incentives can take different forms—aligning your employees' interests with yours or disincentivizing employees from working for your competitors.

With early planning you might include equity ownership as part of your employees' compensation (such as stock options). Later in the life of your business (or on the path to a sale), employees could be offered a "termination bonus" payable if they stay on through closing a sale and even beyond.

The stressful and high-stakes period of selling your business is not the time to encounter difficulties with your employees. Once they become aware of the sale, they are likely to feel insecure at work and may start to look for options. Expect this natural reaction and do what you can to mitigate this risk — get started years in advance.

Later in this book, I will address the art of dealing with employees so that you can make them an asset to your sale and not the source of an internal meltdown. Most employees should be notified of a sale as late as possible—even on the closing day. Others must know of the sale early to facilitate the process or be interviewed in the buyer's due diligence.

Conduct Your Own Due Diligence

As a sale becomes foreseeable, owners should conduct "due diligence" on their own business. **Don't let the first due diligence of your business be performed by the attorney and other advisors working for the company that acquires you.**

Be sure your company is properly qualified to do business in all the states where it maintains a physical presence (or a sufficient legal "nexus"). Review your corporate minutes, tax returns, and intellectual property records. Keep close records of all your major contracts and make note of all clauses that require consent to assignment. Conduct an analysis of Strengths, Weaknesses, Opportunities, and Threats on a regular basis where you identify your market share, market size and trends, organizational goals and values, and competitive advantages.

Be mindful of the rigorous process a business owner must endure to sell a company. It makes sense and generates the highest price for your business to start the long process of planning to sell on the first day your business is formed.

Zack, Southern Electrical Supplies

Prior to incorporating SES, Zack spoke again with his mentor at the SBA and he consulted with a CPA, a partner at Sells & Staff. Then, Zack paid for professional services prior to incorporating SES. His new CPA referred him to a corporate attorney who assisted him with the incorporation of SES as a subchapter S corporation.

Zack borrowed $150,000 from his parents to capitalize SES. He repaid this personal loan, with interest, over a five-year payment schedule.

Through the first two years of SES's operations, Zack's wife, Kelly, handled all the bookkeeping, administrative, and basic legal matters. Kelly previously worked as the administrator of a medical office, so she was well-qualified to handle these tasks. Kelly used a common accounting program to keep the books, manage payables and invoice customers.

Zack was surprised at the cost of liability insurance and workers' compensation. With Zach being young and in good health, SES

---

invested in a key man life insurance policy to provide for Kelly if he died. His corporate attorney recommended that he start to plan for his corporate succession if something were to happen to him. SES's initial board of directors was composed of Kelly and Zack. Zack then elected Chris, a key and trusted SES salesman, to his board of directors in order to keep him abreast of major corporate and operational matters.

Being a single-owner S corporation, SES's corporate legal matters were relatively simple. Kelly consulted with SES's corporate attorney for all general business matters, drafting model forms for use with customers and reviewing all of SES's major agreements. SES registered trademarks of its name and logo.

All employees and contractors were required to sign agreements that prevent their use of SES's proprietary information while they work for SES and for three years after they leave SES. All W-2 employees were properly classified as such and paid through an outsourced payroll system, while independent contractors received 1099s each year.

Initially, SES operated out of Zack's house, with all sales and logistics personnel working remotely and inventory stored at a shared warehouse. In 1994, SES leased industrial warehouse and office space, and used its corporate attorney to negotiate the lease. Through strong negotiation, and with SES's demonstrated steady profits, Zack was able to avoid signing a personal guaranty of the lease.

In 1994, SES hired a controller, Ella, and upgraded its accounting software. In 2001, Ella was promoted to CFO and hired an accounting manager to handle accounts payable, accounts receivable, inventory and payroll. Today, SES has an accounting staff of four people.

Since its inception, SES has used Sells & Staff to prepare its tax returns. Sells & Staff provides accounting services, of which approximately 80 percent are tax, 15 percent are attestation services (audits and reviews), and five percent are bookkeeping services. Approximately half of its clients are wealthy individuals and half of its clients are businesses.

Zack still owns 100 percent of the stock of SES. However, in 2005 he paid his corporate attorney to create a "phantom stock plan"—an incentive plan that rewards employees for staying employed through a sale without conferring all the rights of shareholders. Phantom stock has been awarded to four members of management, each of whom remains employed with SES. The phantom stock plan will entitle the four holders of phantom stock to receive an aggregate of 12 percent of the net proceeds from the sale of the company so long as they are employed with SES on the closing date.

SES incurs between $15,000 and $25,000 annually in professional fees charged by its CPA, its corporate attorney, and other attorneys. SES has never been involved in litigation or any government enforcement action.

Harry, Elegant Catering

Harry remembered from a friend in real estate that organizing his business as a limited liability company (LLC) was the "thing to do." Harry contributed $50,000 to the LLC, and Skip agreed to serve as the banquet captain at all major events. Elegant Catering is staffed with a team ranging from 20 to 30 cooks, servers, bartenders and banquet captains. Elegant Catering has always paid everyone as independent contractors, including Harry and Skip.

Being licensed as an attorney, Harry took responsibility for legal and administrative matters. Harry formed the LLC using an online legal document provider. In 2014, two years after Elegant Catering was founded, Harry sought a tax accountant and was referred to an Enrolled Agent, Helen, who was the sister of a fraternity friend. Following Helen's advice, Harry hired a bookkeeper.

Helen had prepared tax returns for only four years. Most of her other clients were individuals, many of whom were Marines at Camp Pendleton. She referred all her business clients to the same bookkeeper because she had never worked with any others. Elegant Catering's bookkeeper had to recreate books for the past two years from disorganized records, even using Harry's personal bank account and credit card statements.

Harry and Skip had a falling out in late 2014, after the initial tax returns were prepared and ensuing arguments erupted over their relative contributions of time to the business. Their dispute spilled over to affect others, impacting business operations and nearly shutting down the company. The LLC's Operating Agreement, provided by an online legal document provider, had no clause governing the buyout of either partner.

Feeling threatened by the fact that Harry was an attorney, Skip hired a business litigator. Harry did the same, since he was not versed in business law. After months of negotiation and over $26,000 in combined legal fees, Harry purchased Skip's ownership interest in the company for $30,000.

Bitter over the cost of legal fees from this dispute, Harry resolved that he would never pay another attorney. Legal issues continued to arise from time to time, but Harry relied upon free advice from a law school classmate who once prepared Harry's estate plan.

For nearly five years, Elegant Catering ran its administrative headquarters in Harry's apartment, with shared access to use the kitchen of a struggling restaurant, which was subsequently evicted by its landlord. Under duress to find kitchen space, in 2016 Harry signed a 10-year lease at rent above the current market rate. Harry signed a personal guaranty with the lease.

Despite the bad blood between Harry and Skip, Harry was able to salvage Elegant Catering's virtual monopoly on events at Bayside Views.

Chapter Two:

ANTICIPATE THE SALE PROCESS

Selling a business is a huge task and preparation is crucial. Completing any form of sale, merger or acquisition transaction is like running a marathon. If your training is delayed by unexpected circumstances months into the process, you can always resume your training. However, if you don't start now your performance will suffer.

Business sales are known by a variety of names: "mergers & acquisitions" (or "M&A"), "change in control" or "reorganization." Some of these labels connote the legal form of the sale transaction, including "asset sale", "merger", and "stock sale". As previously mentioned, this book focuses on the sale of privately-owned businesses and not publicly traded ones.

Sellers entering their first business sale (or M&A transaction) should take extra time to educate themselves. Attaining familiarity with the norms of these transactions will mitigate the risk of making a bad deal or damaging a good one.

Business professionals should help you sell your business. Education and preparation will allow an owner to speak up when the need arises and know when to get out of the way and trust their professionals and advisors.

Before choosing the appropriate exit strategy, advisors should work closely with you to consider your personal circumstances, the condition of your business and the state of the market.

OVERVIEW OF THE SALE PROCESS

Plan for the mechanics and negotiation of the sale. An offer typically will come in a non-binding term sheet or letter of intent (see Appendix B), and often at a high enough price to make you stop looking for other buyers.

Then, the buyer will start its own due diligence and may try to whittle down the price for every issue they find. So, don't let them find any. If the buyer finds too many organizational and legal errors or sees that the accounting is not reliable or as profitable as originally represented, they may walk away. Many sellers have never prepared financial statements in accordance with generally accepted accounting principles (commonly referred to as "GAAP") and do not know the true profits of their business.

In the purchase agreement, the buyer will push all unwanted or uncertain risks onto the seller and will seek to withhold a corresponding portion of the purchase price to secure against the risk of losses. This alone is motivation to maintain better internal controls and an ongoing relationship with corporate legal counsel.

IDENTIFYING A BUYER

Begin with the end in mind: the successful closing of sale to a buyer who greatly values your business.

Envision your ideal buyers and the ones you want to avoid. Be careful dealing with potential acquirers that are also your competitors if they might be seeking information to use against you. There are a range of potential buyers of a closely held business.

Common potential buyers fall into the following categories:

- A financial buyer who values the return on their investment of acquiring your business.
- A strategic buyer, typically another company already operating in your industry and seeking integration or access to new markets.
- Private equity firms.
- Management or leveraged buyouts.
- Family members.
- An Employee Stock Ownership Plan (ESOP).

Confirm with experts that you have reasonable expectations about your future buyer.

YOUR PRIORITIES FOR THE SALE

Identify your priorities about what will distinguish an ideal M&A event from a disappointment. Based on some of the most common concerns of business owners you should consider each of the following:

- The price that should be paid by the buyer.
- How the purchase price will be funded (cash, third party financing, seller promissory notes).
- The after-tax proceeds from the sale.
- Impact of the sale upon employees.
- Family members working in the business.
- The continuing legacy of the business you've spent years building.
- Protection of confidential information before the sale closes.
- Repaying and retiring current business debts and liabilities for which the seller is liable.
- The seller's obligation to provide services to the business after the closing.

After envisioning your ideal buyer and considering your own personal priorities, you can research these issues and plan for a transaction which achieves your goals. You should work with your advisors to develop reasonable expectations about how well you might achieve each of these ends and which ones you are willing to sacrifice.

YOUR VALUATION AND PRICE

Ultimately, the purchase price is the most important factor in your sale, and you must be able to justify the price you hope to receive. You should be prepared to show that your company has quantifiable and defensible support for your targeted purchase price.

Sellers should be able to tell a simple story to prospective buyers that justifies their price and valuation. Before getting deep into details, explain revenue in basic terms: the number of widgets sold and the price per widget. Explain the factors influencing the future of both variables. Tell the story, instead of spinning it.

Your Financial Data and Valuation

Sellers should have credible support for their financial projections and any underlying assumptions. Understand income statement adjustments, particularly add-backs, and study any pro forma financial statements. Know that acquiring companies seek synergy between the two businesses in order to justify a price.

Valuation multiples will reflect the quality of earnings, particularly revenue growth and trends in Earnings Before Interest Taxes Depreciation and Amortization ("EBITDA"). Tax considerations and costs of integration will have a measurable impact on the deal.

Sellers may obtain a professional valuation of the company which could help in negotiations, fulfill fiduciary duties and protect management from claims by outside shareholders. Valuations are usually based upon a comparison of several of the following methods: multiples of EBITDA, multiples of seller's discretionary earnings, comparison with comparable (publicly traded) companies, similar private company M&A transactions, discounted future cash flows and a leveraged buyout analysis.

See more about valuation in Chapter 8.

Differences Between Main Street and Middle-Market Transactions

This book surveys a range of issues relevant to selling a small business or a middle-market business. However, certain aspects of a sale are usually handled differently for small businesses vs. middle-market businesses. These subjects are covered in detail in subsequent chapters, so read on and refer back to this list of differences.

Keep in mind that sellers are wise to cooperate and "go with the flow" rather than disrupting or derailing a potential sale when a buyer's approach to the transaction does not follow the norm.

The Role of Business Brokers/M&A Advisors

With the sale of a small business, the seller is usually represented by a "business broker" who may provide a broader range of services than those provided by an M&A Advisor in a middle-market transaction. This is because other professional service providers (including attorneys and CPAs) usually play a lesser role in small business sales in order to reduce costs. (See Chapter 4.)

The Role of Attorneys

Attorneys often play a reduced role in the sale of a Main Street businesses, and sometimes no role at all. A business broker should encourage parties to have key agreements reviewed by their attorneys, but the sale process can become unduly complicated or expensive by adding a high level of legal analysis and negotiation.

Attorneys are deeply involved in the sale of middle-market businesses: drafting and negotiating agreements, completing due diligence, protecting privileged information, and guiding the sale through to closing. (See Chapters 4 and 11.)

The Letter of Intent

Small businesses are often sold without the execution a letter of intent. Middle-market businesses receive offers in the form of letters of intent, the execution of which begins the sale process and leads to the execution of formal purchase agreements.

Small business sales usually begin with the execution of purchase agreements. The purchase agreement is usually a broker's form with fewer representations and warranties about the business but including contingencies, so the buyer is not bound to purchase a business until completion of due diligence. (See Chapters 5 and 6.)

Valuation/Price Negotiations

With the sale of a small business the seller and business broker estimate the value of the business and usually publicly advertise a selling price. Owners of middle-market businesses should have quantifiable estimates of their value, but the potential buyers usually initiate the price negotiations with an offer. (See Chapter 8.)

Purchase Agreement

In the sale of a small business the purchase agreement is usually a form document with limited representations and warranties about the business, but including contingencies for the buyer to obtain financing, complete due diligence, assume the lease, transfer the franchise, and similar events necessary to close the sale.

The purchase agreement for a middle-market business is tailored to the transaction and the business being sold, requiring more drafting and negotiation by attorneys. The buyer will want more disclosure about the business and protection against future claims arising from the seller's operation of the business. (See Chapter 11.)

Timing and Scope of Due Diligence

In all cases, execution of a nondisclosure agreement precedes delivery of any information. Nearly all buyers will require financial statements before they will make an offer. In the sale of a small business due diligence often follows the execution of a purchase agreement.

For the sale of a middle-market business, most due diligence is completed during the period between the execution of a letter of intent and the execution of a purchase agreement. Due diligence is usually conducted while the purchase agreement is drafted by attorneys. Due diligence is far broader and deeper in the sale of middle-market businesses with more participation by attorneys and other advisors. (See Chapter 12.)

Financing

Main Street business sales are generally financed with loans guaranteed by the SBA and seller financing. Middle-market sales typically have far more financing alternatives. (See Chapter 10.)

ZACK, SOUTHERN ELECTRICAL SUPPLIES

In 2017, Zack realized he was working too many hours to spend time with his children during their final years at home, and he believed that construction was "at the top" of the market cycle. Like many business owners, he first discussed the idea of selling his business with his CPA at Sells & Staff. He had also spoken to his uncle who sold a construction framing business and other entrepreneurs and mentors he knew through the SBA.

According to Zack's CPA, SES was generating EBITDA of roughly $3 million per year, and the company had no debt. At a conservative multiple of five times EBITDA, SES might sell for approximately $15 million. SES was well-established, stable and financially healthy, so Zack had little doubt that SES could outlive its founder. SES had grown large enough that Zack would receive proceeds from the sale — after payments owed on the phantom stock plan, the costs of the sale, and all taxes — to retire comfortably.

Zack consulted with his CPA to develop an expectation of the tax liability he would incur if he sold the business in an asset sale and they considered how he could best allocate the purchase price among the assets of the business. Zack worked with his wealth

---

advisor, CPA and corporate lawyer to confirm the best path to mitigate the taxable gain.

Zack spoke to SES's corporate attorney who confirmed he had enough experience representing sellers of middle-market businesses. He spoke with several business brokers, M&A advisors and investment bankers about the alternative methods to attract a buyer.

Ultimately, Zack hired an M&A advisor who could represent him through the process of considering his alternative exit strategies, preparing the business for sale, marketing and/or listing the business for sale, identifying a buyer and completing the sale process.

Zack undertook preparations immediately, working with his M&A advisor, financial advisors, CPA and corporate attorney. Zack's wealth advisor perked up when learning that Zack's net worth would move from his ownership of SES into liquid assets requiring management. Zack told his wealth advisor that he hoped to sell SES within two years.

HARRY, ELEGANT CATERING

In 2017, Harry met the love of his life, Nilufer, who made a substantially higher income than Harry as a merchant banker for Rothschild in Manhattan. After dating long-distance for nearly a year, he and Nil decided to unite in New York.

Elegant Catering's business operations suffered when Harry was away on extended trips to New York. Harry knew that he could not rely on any of his banquet captains to manage the business. He needed to sell to save his relationship and hopes of marrying Nil.

In January 2018, Harry called a business broker who promised that he could sell Elegant Catering in four months. Harry immediately signed an exclusive listing agreement with a business broker who would receive a fee equal to 10% of the total sales price. Harry directed his business broker to sell Elegant Catering for $2.5 million, a sum chosen to make him financially secure for the foreseeable future.

Chapter Three:

HOW AND WHEN TO MARKET YOUR BUSINESS FOR SALE

After determining your priorities for selling your business, you can plan to execute a transaction which achieves your goals. You should work with your advisors to develop reasonable expectations about how to achieve each of these ends and which ones you are willing to sacrifice.

Some businesses might sell at an early stage, particularly if the seller fits a business need for a strategic buyer—another company in the same industry. However, most businesses require several years of consistent operations to demonstrate the income-generating capacity of the business. The general rule is that the best time to sell is when your business is thriving and generating cash without being overly dependent upon your services to the company.

You will need to implement the optimal sale process at the right time, identify the right buyer and command the right price.

Choosing Your Ideal Sale Process

Using realistic expectations about how to achieve your goals, you should determine the appropriate sales process based upon expected timing, management resources, the number and nature of potential buyers and the desired level of confidentiality. Marketing your business for sale directly to a greater number of buyers will lead to a longer process and may reduce the level of confidentiality you are able to maintain.

- A negotiated sale typically involves one to three potential buyers;
- A targeted high-level solicitation typically involves three to 10 potential buyers;
- A targeted auction, a sale with 10 to 20 potential buyers; and
- A broad auction, a sale with 30 or more potential buyers.

Even a seller who expects to conduct a broad auction should categorize the suitability of buyers. Consider whether to approach potential buyers in tiers, starting with the buyers who are most likely to say "no." It will be crucial to screen out unqualified buyers to make better use of your resources and protect confidential information.

The primary objective is to increase the value, appeal and marketability of your business with the goal of generating multiple competing bids to acquire your business: create a "seller's market".

MARKETING AND PROMOTING YOUR BUSINESS FOR SALE

After judging the broader market conditions, you can plan how to promote your business to potential buyers. Plan for the techniques you will use to market your business for sale and the information you will share with prospective buyers.

The Marketing Approach

You should work with your advisors to determine the appropriate method to identify a buyer. The ideal approach for marketing a business for sale runs the gamut.

Will you use a business broker or an M&A advisor to list the business for sale on standard listing services? Will you be able to find a buyer through targeting ideal strategic buyers you have identified? Will you "pitch" your business for sale to sophisticated investors like private equity groups or family offices? Will you consummate an internal transfer to management, family members or employees? Will a business broker, investment banker or M&A advisor promote your business to a targeted group?

Investment Bankers and Business Brokers

Large Wall Street investment bankers support transactions with a minimum price of $50 million to $100 million. Smaller investment banks will service transactions of at least $10 million. If you own a small to mid-sized business of several hundred thousand dollars to $5 million, you will either use a business broker, M&A advisor or try to sell the business yourself.

Investment bankers and business brokers offer advantages over attempting to sell your own business:

- An investment banker or business broker has knowledge of the pool of potential buyers.
- Since this advisor has more knowledge of potential buyers and resources for identifying prospective buyers, they will be able to find multiple prospects and permit an auction of your business.
- They will be able to screen potential buyers, focusing your time on ones who are serious and financially capable of closing a sale.
- They will facilitate early discussions about your business while maintaining confidentiality with prospective buyers.
- They have deal experience, guiding you through the negotiations and completion of the sale, keeping all parties' expectations realistic and their actions on a path to close.

Investment bankers and business brokers typically earn a success fee upon the closing of the sale. A business broker typically earns 10% of the sale price up to $500,000 or $1,000,000 and a lower percentage on the sale price above the first $1,000,000. An investment banker usually charges a lower percentage (4% to 6%) since the selling prices of the companies they represent are higher. Wall Street investment banks traditionally followed a fee structure called the Double Lehman or Modern Lehman formula which is applied to calculate fees on a sell-side engagement as follows:

- 10% of the first $1 million
- 8% of the second $1 million
- 6% of the third $1 million
- 4% of the fourth $1 million, and
- 2% of everything above $4 million.

Due to inflation, large investment banks have changed their formulas, switching to $10 million increments.

Selling Yourself

Just like homeowners may sell by themselves, business owners can sell without the help of a broker or banker. Maintaining confidentiality of your decision to sell is far more difficult if you don't use such an advisor. In communications sent to prospective buyers, you must anonymize your business and designate a trusted advisor (such as your accountant or attorney) to receive inquiries.

The most difficult challenge will be the identification of a buyer. You should use an attorney or accountant to consult with investment bankers and business brokers who represent potential buyers, advertise in trade journals or business newspapers, and send letters to companies you believe would be interested (i.e., strategic buyers in your industry).

You might target a company in your industry which has recently completed an initial public offering and lists future acquisitions under the "Use of Proceeds" in its prospectus. This could be a daunting challenge without a broker or banker.

A Marketing Brochure

In addition to determining the method for marketing your business, you will need to deliver the information enticing the buyer to purchase your company. This will be in the form of a marketing brochure, like a "private placement memorandum" for a securities offering. Your business broker or investment banker should take the lead preparing the brochure used to sell your business.

Focus on the factors which are important to buyers and the nature of the content. Your marketing brochure will include a meaningful description of all the key features of your business and financial information, including recent financial statements. A good brochure may take time to prepare and will emphasize your competitive strengths and customer relationships in your market. Your brochure should only be delivered to prospective buyers after a confidentiality agreement has been signed.

Is Your Business Unique or Superior to the Competition?

The competitive standing of your business will dictate whether you can sell in a buyer's market or a seller's market. Most business owners are ignorant of their competitive position in their own industry. It is useful to prepare the marketing brochure years before your sale target date to identify your strengths and weaknesses. In the interim, work to eliminate those weaknesses.

Your business might be so unique or may dominate over your competition, creating a seller's market with multiple buyers bidding for the purchase. You don't want to find yourself in a buyer's market where you compete with other sellers for an offer from one ideal buyer.

Many businesses are not viewed as unique, possibly because they have not put in the effort to distinguish themselves from their competition. These businesses run the risk of being viewed as a "commodity". This can cause a general disregard for anything that might be considered unique about your business, coupled with a lack of recognition or appreciation for any characteristics of the business that might give the buyer a competitive advantage in future operations. This scenario will often drive down the purchase price by pitting one seller against the other, with the business ultimately being acquired by the lowest bidder.

KNOW THE CURRENT CONDITIONS IN THE BROADER MARKET

"It's the Economy, Stupid."

An important part of the exit strategy process is to consider the prevailing business climate and whether the eventual date you begin to market your business will occur during a buyer's or a seller's market based upon a broad measure of economic conditions. This will impact whether you will be able to achieve the sales price you desire.

At the time of publication, we are enjoying a long-standing positive trend of strong economic growth, high returns in the stock market which are pushing all the major market indices to historical highs, low interest rates and low unemployment. However, the market for selling a business is not precisely the same as the stock market.

The market for buying and selling a business moves through cycles, and market timing is crucial.

> Market timing is no less important than personal and business timing. There are opportunities to transfer a business in almost any type of economy. The unexpected knock on the door from an overpaying consolidator, however, happens only to the guy three lockers down. Everyone else must increase their market savvy to realize their goals. To maximize a transfer, a healthy transfer market is a good place to start. The U.S. transfer market seems to run in ten-year cycles, as shown [below].
>
> Deal periods in a transfer cycle are not binary switches. Rather, they are like leaky deal faucets. There are opportunities in every period for an owner to create and maximize an exit. However, sellers are most likely to get a good deal in [a] seller's market.[3]

The market for buying and selling businesses has shown a ten-year cycle (see Figure 3.1).

UNITED STATES TEN YEAR PRIVATE TRANSFER CYCLE[4]

Buyer's Market	Seller's Market	Uncertain Market

1980	1983	1988	1990
1990	1993	1998	2000
2000	2003	2008	2010
2010	2013	2018	2020

Acquire Companies   **Divest Companies**

Figure 3.1[4]

However, economic and financial conditions for buyers drive the market. Look to the cash reserves held by private equity firms and publicly traded companies to find indicators of the current climate for a business sale.

THE EFFECT OF BABY BOOMER BUSINESS SELLERS

For years, market observers have predicted a "tsunami" of business sales due to the retirement of baby boomers. Estimates of the impact of retiring baby boomers have ranged from an additional 200,000 to nearly 400,000 businesses marketed for sale each year.

Baby boomers, Americans born between 1946 and 1964, own approximately two-thirds of businesses in the U.S. — roughly four million companies. Assuming 65 is the average retirement age in the United States, baby boomers began to retire in 2011.

Retiring Boomers have impacted the market but not nearly as much as anticipated:

> This predicted "tsunami" of businesses for sale relied on the law of supply and demand to suggest business valuations would plummet and be difficult to sell. Owners were advised to sell fast before the value of their business, and the majority of their net worth, collapsed.[5]

Data compiled by market analyst PitchBook indicates that the number of middle-market businesses put up for sale has increased since 2011, but the number of transactions which ultimately closed has increased at a higher rate. "Despite a large increase in sellers in the market, valuations have remained steady, even increasing 4 percent in 2015," said PitchBook analyst Daniel Cook.

> The predictions assumed the majority of the 4 million boomer businesses would enter the market in an attempt to sell to a third party. "About 70 percent of our members' clients do not choose to market their business to third party buyers," said John Brown, CEO of Denver-based BEI... "In most cases, our clients transfer the business to their children or employees."[6]

You should consider the fact that retiring baby boomers will place their businesses up for sale through 2030, creating more competition among sellers. This is yet another reason to start planning, preparing and selling your business.

Your Age and Health

Selling a business and living a prosperous retirement is the American dream. Dying behind your desk and leaving a fire sale for your executor is a nightmare. If the point hasn't be reinforced enough, start planning early to target a date for the sale.

Selling a business will require energy and push you to your limits and selling while your business is thriving will usually require your most active engagement. Your first attempt to sell might not generate the interest or price you seek, and you might need to abort and try again later.

You can never be guaranteed that your health will be strong until a given date, so your target sale date should be several years before you must sell. Ideally, the right time to sell is when your business is generating profits, your industry is thriving, and the economy is strong.

Speak with a business broker, investment banker or M&A advisor and determine the right time and the right process for selling your business. Find the proper way to market your business as one that is unique and generate a seller's market.

ZACK, SOUTHERN ELECTRICAL SUPPLIES

Zack and his M&A advisor completed a thorough process reviewing all his exit strategy alternatives considering Zack's personal needs, the condition of the business and the state of the market. He was 58, had family reasons to sell and knew the process could take years. SES was in excellent condition with a strong market for selling a construction-related supply business.

No members of Zack's family worked for SES, the individual members of management lacked the financial wherewithal and entrepreneurial expertise to acquire SES, and Zack wasn't interested in remaining active in the business through a partial acquisition by a private equity group. An employee stock ownership plan (ESOP) was a viable alternative. Although a strategic buyer seemed like the most likely acquirer, Zack preferred to see SES continue as a stand-alone business under the name and reputation he built.

Since SES had developed such a strong brand, even a strategic buyer was likely to keep its trade name. Zack understood that a strategic buyer was his best alternative. Since the sale price was likely to exceed $10 million, Zack agreed to pay his M&A advisor a fee based on a sliding scale between 4% and 6%.

In 2017, the broader market for business sales was strong. Zack elected to have SES marketed for sale through major listing services and directly to potential buyers including the pool of potential buyers known by his M&A advisor. If SES didn't sell to an independent buyer, SES could retain consultants with expertise in ESOP transactions.

SES worked with its CPA to prepare GAAP financial statements. Zack worked with his M&A advisor to draft a brochure, much like a private placement memorandum or prospectus that highlighted the strengths of SES and its steady profitability. He reduced his workload to spend more time with his family before the sale process escalated. He was in good health and could work for another 10 years if necessary.

HARRY, ELEGANT CATERING

Harry envisioned that his buyer would be an entrepreneur with experience in catering, restaurants or managing an event property, much like himself. After listing Elegant Catering in 2018, Harry began to spend more time with Nilufer in New York. Operations began to suffer, and profits fell. His Enrolled Agent, Helen, had always extended the filing of his tax returns, but now fell two years behind.

Harry directed his business broker to sell Elegant Catering for $2.5 million so that Harry would not need to work after the sale. However, at only 38, Harry would still need to work again to sustain himself through retirement. Without current tax returns, Harry lacked any financial statements to support an asking price of $2.5 million.

Harry reviewed his anonymous business listing which made his business look stable, although he knew the financial data was not current.

Three months after Elegant Catering was listed for sale, Harry had heard nothing from his broker about any buyer interest. However, Harry never asked how his broker was marketing Elegant Catering for sale. His broker was simply relying upon a listing to generate buyer interest. His broker had no pre-existing relationships with any prospective buyers. After several heated calls with his business broker, Harry's broker advised him to lower the price. He initially resisted, but ultimately agreed to lower the price to $2 million.

Chapter Four:

THE M&A TEAM YOU NEED

No one who wants to sell their business for top dollar should go through the process without professional assistance. Many of the members of your "M&A Team" are already working for you: your CPA, corporate attorney and wealth advisor. Be sure that each of them is qualified to work on an M&A transaction.

You need not hire Goldman Sachs and a PricewaterhouseCoopers, but this is not the time to skimp. Save money on professional fees by being prepared and avoiding the need to redo work. The earlier you can begin the sale process, the better that you and your M&A Team (see Figure 5.1) can manage the necessary work and save money on fees.

Your first step should be to assemble an outstanding professional team to advise you. Most businesspeople select their professional team on the eve of their sale. This is far too late in the sale process. By selecting your professional team several years before the target date for your sale, you can obtain their guidance in the presale years as to methods of minimizing the obstacles.[7]

YOUR M&A TEAM

Member	Role	Objectives
The Owner	Vision and final decisions.	Continue to increase sales, improve efficiencies and boost company value. Assemble and oversee M&A Team.
M&A Advisor or investment banker	Advice about the sales process and potential buyers.	Find the best buyer for your business, lead the negotiations, facilitate the sale, and coordinate the M&A Team's efforts.
Attorney	Legal.	Legal strategy, agreements and advice. Minimize risk and liability exposure.
CPA/Tax Advisor	Tax planning and advice.	Minimize your tax liabilities from the sale of your business.
Wealth Manager	Personal financial advice.	Wealth management and budgeting. Help you determine a minimum sale price necessary to meet post-sale financial objectives.
Appraiser (if needed)	Appraise the company.	Determine the value of the business.
Banker	Financing.	Assist with immediate and long-term capital needs and lending activities.

Figure 5.1

Do not assemble a group of "yes men" who agree with every thought you share. Build a team of qualified professionals who will ask the tough questions before the buyer does.

M&A Advisor, Investment Banker or Business Broker

An individual serving as an M&A advisor, investment banker or business broker will take the most central and broadest role to facilitate the sale of your business. Whatever their title, your M&A advisor will serve the business in an oversight role, often coordinating the services of the rest of your M&A Team and doing more to market your business than simply listing it on the various listing services.

If your business is sold in a securities transaction, an investment banker with securities licenses may be necessary to fill this role.

> They act as sage counsel, uncover a large universe of buyers, run your auction, take on the role of the bad guy so the business owner doesn't have to. They run great interference and know how to play buyers off against one another to get you the absolute best deal. And they normally can smoke out when a buyer is not real, which can save you huge amounts of time and money. ... Remember, their fees are nearly all success based. They only get real money if you get real money.[8]

ATTORNEY

You should not wait for the drafting of a purchase agreement to bring a qualified M&A attorney into the loop. Be sure your M&A attorney is a corporate transactional lawyer with extensive experience in mergers & acquisitions. Your M&A attorney should be involved before you execute a letter of intent, and the earlier you have your attorney involved, the more value you will derive from his or her services.

Your attorney shouldn't merely draft agreements. He or she should help you to structure this transaction in the best way to serve your interests. If your attorney joins the Team after a deal has been agreed upon, the structure might strongly favor the buyer.

No document, contract or agreement should be signed throughout the exit process without the review, input and advice from your M&A attorney. Your attorney should participate in the due diligence process to take any necessary corrective action discovered through due diligence (e.g., reviewing or amending contracts), help protect your confidential information and sort out disagreements with the buyer.

TAX ADVISOR

The services of your CPA (and possibly additional tax advisors) are necessary so that you don't pay any more taxes to the state and federal government than necessary. Your sale may trigger a number of tax issues:

- Federal income taxes
- State income taxes
- State sales and use taxes
- Final payroll taxes and withholdings
- Real estate tax reassessments
- Personal property tax reassessments
- International taxes
- State documentary and transfer fees

Tax strategy is usually a critical part of the exit strategy process. Business owners often assume they will receive capital gains treatment on 100% of the sale proceeds. Sellers are frequently surprised to discover that material portions of the transaction are taxed as ordinary income, such as the recapture of accumulated depreciation.

Early planning may alter the tax treatment of the proceeds from the sale. If you are organized as a C corporation, you may face two layers of taxation and wish to allocate a portion of the purchase price to a consulting agreement or to the personal goodwill of the owner.

WEALTH ADVISOR

Many business owners wait until the sale closes before consulting with their wealth advisor about their options to invest the proceeds from the sale and develop a long-term financial strategy. This delay in engaging the advice of a wealth advisor could be the costliest mistake a business owner will make during the exit strategy process.

Wealth advisors should be drafted into your M&A Team early in the process. He or she needs to work directly with the attorney, tax specialists and others on the M&A Team. Your wealth manager also needs to know if the purchase price will be paid in cash or if you will carry a note receivable. Your advisor needs to know the estimated value of your assets that will be available after taxes to provide for your financial future.

Your wealth advisor should be one of the more financially savvy members of your M&A Team. Thus, they may help to validate the key issues of whether you are selling for a high enough price and whether the proceeds from the sale will last through your retirement.

How much is enough to retire? The answer is specific for each seller, their lifestyle and their assets outside of the business. Depending on their need for income, and considering expected returns and variability of investments, a talented wealth advisor can help the business owner determine how much capital is required to retire.

Your target retirement sum is essentially whatever amount of assets, net of taxes and fees, allow you to replace your business income, and possibly endow you to live the rest of your life on an after-tax, after-inflation basis, to make sure you never run out of money. Factors like current expenses, plans for additional purchases, debt balances, and desires for gifting to family and philanthropic entities are critical.

Your financial advisor needs to spend time with you to determine your post-sale goals and needs in order to ensure that you will be able to accomplish those goals and fulfill those needs. A capable wealth advisor will have appropriate tools to run multiple scenarios to help you evaluate tradeoffs between risks and rewards along their path to wealth protection and lifestyle maintenance, and even more so to make sure the path is comfortable, and that your more important life goals have the highest probabilities of coming to fruition.

Once you and your wealth advisor have determined how much is "enough", you can work with your other advisors to push for the terms that work best in this context, and even to develop preferences about which potential buyer might represent the better steward of the business you have built.

Do not look solely to the sum you need to retire when assessing your sale price. Demanding an excessive sale price—for any reason—is the primary impediment to selling a business.

Prior to closing, you should have a game plan for the short-term investment of the sale proceeds. The funds should be invested immediately to avoid the loss of interest.

BANKERS

Bankers are seasoned business advisors. Many have seen their customers go through an exit strategy or other liquidation events.

One of the key principles in this book is the concept of improving sales and profit numbers to increase your company's valuation prior to the sale. Bankers understand that increased sales will generally cause increases in accounts receivable, inventory, fixed assets, and overhead, which can often lead to a decrease in available cash. Bankers can assist your company with this financial challenge by helping you increase available cash through lines of credit and other loan instruments.

A banker should be a valuable resource assisting the buyer with the financing of the transaction and the closing of the sale. However, the buyer will typically have its own banking relationships as discussed in Chapter 10 on Financing the Sale.

Retain or engage all the necessary members of your M&A Team. Understand their proper roles. Start their work early. Keep their efforts coordinated and maintain an appropriate level of oversight to control the process while you continue to manage a thriving business.

KEY EMPLOYEES

In addition to your M&A Team, your key employees can be crucial in preparing for a sale, completing the sale and ensuring the buyer's successful transition into ownership of your business. The art is to get assistance from your employees without revealing that your business is for sale.

Your key employees may eventually hear about your plans to sell the business. Some of their immediate concerns might be:

- Job insecurity and potential changes to their status in the company.
- Their inability to work for you in the future.
- Transformation of the company culture resulting from new ownership.
- Possible changes in salary or benefits.

The success or failure of your sale could depend upon your key employees. The buyer may want to speak with key management before closing. Some of these key personnel will become an important part of the sale process and the transition subsequent to the close of the sale.

Timing the disclosure of the sale is crucial to keep the deal on track while you limit disclosure to those who need to know and keep your business operating successfully. Small business owners should usually wait until after closing to disclose the sale to employees. Seek input from your M&A Team to balance these conflicting factors.

ZACK, SOUTHERN ELECTRICAL SUPPLIES

Since the beginning of SES, Zack was served by a CPA and corporate attorney who were qualified to represent SES from its founding to his sale. This helped to eliminate problems through the growth of SES and made for good "institutional knowledge" when he began to sell. Zack's M&A advisor worked well with his CPA and corporate attorney.

Zack's wealth advisor and CPA consulted about ways to defer the recognition of the gain from sale, including a charitable remainder trust and retirement account alternatives. SES's CPA and corporate attorney advised Zack that he might be able to reorganize the corporate structure of SES and implement a pension plan to offset much of the gain on the sale. Zack's CPA referred him to a specialist in defined benefit plans. Ultimately,

---

Zack reorganized SES's corporate structure and implemented a defined benefit plan.

To date, Zack's wealth advisor had minimal responsibilities beyond advising Zack about his 401(k) plan, 529 college savings accounts for his children, life insurance and discretionary investing accounts. Zack reinvested most of the profits from SES into the business, making it the overwhelming majority of his net worth.

After exploring ideas to improve SES's profits, Zack established a line of credit with a banker recommended by his CPA. SES was able to borrow in order to invest in a branding program and enhanced inventory and logistics management.

Zack's CPA and attorney confirmed that his M&A advisor (who was licensed as a broker and appraiser) had provided him a professional valuation of SES. His M&A advisor also identified an independent valuation firm that could provide an independent valuation if necessary. Since Zack was the sole shareholder of SES, and he received professional confirmation of the valuation received from his M&A advisor, he elected to forego a valuation from an independent firm.

HARRY, ELEGANT CATERING

Three months after listing Elegant Catering for sale and receiving no buyer interest, Harry followed his broker's advice and lowered the sale price from $2.5 million to $2 million. Still, Harry had no financial statements that he could provide to potential buyers to substantiate his asking price.

Harry was concerned about the status of his delinquent tax returns. Helen was difficult to reach, and when he finally reached her, she explained that Harry's bookkeeper had fallen behind in her work due to health and personal problems.

In October 2018, Harry received two notices regarding the employment classification of his catering staff, one from the California Employment Development Department and one from the IRS. A disgruntled part-time cook reported Elegant Catering's employment practices to both agencies. Harry called his Enrolled Agent for help with this problem but soon realized she was not capable of helping him resolve it.

Harry was forced to call an employment attorney he knew from law school. Although she had been recently promoted to partner, she was required to take a retainer of $5,000 to help Harry with this employee misclassification issue.

Harry's conversations with his business broker were usually brief, where his broker would notify him that he had not received any serious indications of interest, only a few flaky prospective buyers who were pursuing several businesses at once but lacked financial resources and business experience.

Harry remembered the 10-year, above-market lease which would not expire until 2026, which he personally guaranteed, and he began to feel financial pressure. In the meantime, several other major catering businesses were thriving in Dana Point, California. The management of Bayside Views grew frustrated with Elegant Catering's services and Harry's absence from town.

Chapter Five:

THE LENGTHY NEGOTIATION AND SALE PROCESS

You've gauged the market, reached the decision to sell your company, become familiar with valuation methods, earnings metrics and alternative processes for selling, envisioned an ideal buyer, and assembled your M&A Team. Now you can draft a roadmap with a timeline. Sellers should also familiarize themselves with the fundamental deal terms to be negotiated with the buyer and develop a strategy for negotiating.

POTENTIAL BUYERS

Potential buyers can be classified as financial buyers, strategic buyers and those who fall into neither category.

Financial Buyers

A financial buyer is motivated by financial considerations, the operating results, profitability and financial condition of your business. A financial buyer is not buying your business to realize synergies with an existing business (unless they would combine your business with a larger, existing business).

You may receive a lower price from a financial buyer, but this isn't always the case. If a financial buyer is heavily capitalized and needs to deploy its funds, such a buyer may be willing to bid a higher price. Financial buyers often pay a portion of the price through a promissory note, which is subordinated to debt they owe to their institutional lenders.

Strategic Buyers

A strategic buyer seeks to acquire your business to realize synergies with its existing business. Strategic buyers look beyond your own operating results and consider the cost savings accompanying their access to new markets. Your operating results are combined with the buyer's operating results and adjusted for savings. A strategic buyer is considering pro forma profitability post-closing and typically takes a longer-term view of the acquisition.

Strategic buyers are usually part of your industry and often competitors. You should be mindful to prevent sharing information with a strategic buyer who is really on a fishing expedition. Your M&A Advisor or business broker should vet prospective buyers, but always be careful sharing information with a competitor.

Other Buyers

Some buyers fall into neither category. A parent may purchase a business for their child or a "serial entrepreneur" may buy your business after selling their own. One partner may purchase the interest of another. You may structure an internal or family succession.

It is crucial to tailor your negotiating strategy to the unique needs of one of these buyers. Your expectations about a realistic selling price may vary widely depending upon the nature of the "other buyer".

DEVELOP A TIMEFRAME

Under ideal circumstances a business can be sold in approximately four to six months. However, often the sale process can last for up to a year or more. For illustrative purposes, the following hypothetical sale is condensed into a four-month time frame. This hypothetical assumes a directed marketing effort of a middle-market business, not reliance upon a business listing.

During the first four weeks, sellers should conduct internal due diligence and prepare marketing materials for a list of potential buyers. Sellers should make timely efforts to avoid simple mistakes by assembling complete corporate minutes, contracts and financial statements. They should also make sure that all contracts are fully executed. Don't look unprofessional when prospective buyers are ready to initiate a deal.

Weeks three through seven are when you will make initial contacts with buyers and distribute marketing materials. In weeks eight through 10, sellers deliver marketing presentations to targeted buyers and review any proposals from buyers.

Upon receipt of the first offer from a buyer, a seller should ask for up to 15 days to formally respond. Take the time for consultation with legal counsel and other advisors and for drafting a thoughtful counteroffer. This is crucial to build a record showing diligence and fiduciary care.

Completing the Sale Process

In weeks 10 through 14, the seller may select the best offer, and such a buyer would conduct due diligence on the company. The lawyers working for the buyer should circulate a draft of the purchase agreement. Finally, in weeks 14 through 16, the parties finalize and sign definitive agreements.

After the purchase agreement is signed, the buyer would complete any remaining due diligence. Issues discovered during due diligence may require corrective action. Ancillary contracts related to the transfer of your business will be negotiated and finalized. All the conditions to closing must be satisfied or waived and the sale may then close.

Weeks if Four Months to Close (Weeks if Six Months to Close)	Actions and Milestones
Weeks One to Four	Internal Due Diligence Prepare Marketing Materials
Weeks Three to Seven (Five to 12)	Initial Contacts with Buyers Distribute Marketing Materials
Weeks Eight to 10 (13 to 16)	Presentations to Targeted Buyers Review Proposals
Weeks 10 to 14 (17 to 20)	Review Offers Negotiate Major Terms Sign Letter of Intent Preliminary Due Diligence
Weeks 14 to 16 (21 to 24)	Complete Due Diligence Sign Purchase Agreement Close the Sale

As a seller, you might benefit by simultaneously signing the purchase agreement and closing the sale so that your business is not tied up indefinitely while the buyer effectively holds an option to close the sale. This subject is discussed in greater detail in Chapter 11.

The parties to the sale will typically maintain an ongoing business relationship for up to a year or more after the sale is closed.

Negotiating the Terms of the Deal

The major deal terms for negotiation are described in this section.

> Any profitable business can be sold. It's just a matter of value, terms and structure. Total company value is not always equal to the cash received at the close of the sale of the business.[9]

The Structure of the Sale

Several deal terms will be negotiated at the initial stage. Your company may be sold through an asset sale or a stock sale. For privately-owned, small or middle-market companies, buyers generally prefer an asset sale to avoid the seller's liabilities and take a stepped-up basis in the assets. This is one good reason why most businesses should be a "flow-through" entity for taxes (generally an S corporation or LLC).

Sellers usually prefer a stock sale in order to transfer the company's liabilities and get capital gain treatment on their stock.

A transaction may also be structured as a merger, which could take the form of a forward merger, a reverse merger, a triangular merger or reverse-triangular merger. More details about the alternative structures of sales are set forth in Chapter 11.

Payment of the Purchase Price

The purchase price is obviously a significant term of the deal, and the form of "consideration" delivered by the buyer to pay the price is of utmost importance. Will the buyer pay the purchase price in cash, stock, a promissory note, or some combination thereof?

Setting an unreasonably high sales price for a small business is more likely to deter prospective buyers than it is to lead to a successful sale. Your business broker should provide detailed guidance on setting your asking price. Depending on your business size and situation, you might not want to fix an asking price so that the price can be tailored to the prospective buyer after you receive feedback from "the market".

You should also consult with your attorney and tax advisor before agreeing upon the structure of your sale and the form of payment of the purchase price. In cash transactions, the parties should focus upon the actual net proceeds to be delivered at closing. The buyer will usually retain a portion of the purchase price as a "holdback" to be paid a year or more after closing. The seller could request that such funds be held in escrow.

The net cash proceeds will reflect transaction costs (including bankers, lawyers, consent payments, etc.) and any immediate tax liabilities. The buyer will usually expect that a portion of the purchase price be used to retire all interest-bearing debt on the target company's books.

For middle-market businesses, the buyer and seller often agree upon a purchase price assuming a given "net working capital" balance — current assets minus current liabilities. If the actual net working capital on the closing date differs materially from the assumed balance, the purchase price will be adjusted. Such adjustments for actual closing date balances of debt and net working capital are often completed after the closing.

Earn-outs

The buyer might want to structure a portion of the purchase price as an "earn-out," contingent upon the future operating results of the acquired business. A seller should remember two general rules related to earn-outs.

First, do not assume you will ever receive the earn-out. Second, strive to base any earn-out upon the company's future revenue (or sales), not EBITDA (earnings before interest, taxes, depreciation and amortization). After closing, the buyer will control future costs and take over accounting, which can lead to disagreements over many expense line items.

An earn-out can be useful when the buyer and seller have differing valuations of the business. If your projections about the future earnings of the business are realized, you should be rewarded for bearing this risk with an aggregate purchase price above what you would receive with a 100% fixed price. Negotiate the terms of the buyout to protect yourself against the buyer's manipulation of earnings and allow averaging of income over multiple earn-out periods.

If you would not accept an offered purchase price without the earn-out component, reconsider whether this is the best offer you can get.

Negotiating Strategy

It is often wise to leave the direct negotiation to an investment banker or business broker. You will have less experience than your professional. You should try to remain above the fray and not engage in direct negotiations with a strategic buyer.

Be mindful of various types of negotiators ranging from a co-operative negotiator who recognizes mutual problems and proposes creative solutions to competitive negotiators with "make or break" demands and threats to walk from the deal.

Buyers to Avoid

As negotiations progress, you may find reasons to terminate negotiations with the following prospective buyers:

- Those who lack the financial resources to buy.
- A strategic buyer on a fishing expedition.
- A buyer where the CEO is not committed to the sale or never engages in negotiations.
- A strategic buyer that lacks prior acquisition experience which is less likely to close.

Protecting Your Business through the Sale

Your decision to sell should be kept confidential. You should maintain the confidentiality of your decisions by limiting any information about your sale to trusted advisors (attorneys, accountants, investment bankers or business brokers), requiring your advisors to only approach potential buyers on a "no-name basis" (keeping your identity confidential) and require potential buyers to sign a confidentiality agreement.

Through the sale, you should protect your proprietary information. Give buyers only enough information to make a purchase decision. Require potential buyers to sign a confidentiality agreement. (A standard non-disclosure agreement is included as Appendix A.) Lastly, you should prohibit potential buyers from hiring away your key employees for a specified period, typically one year.

Each of the key aspects of the sale process is described in detail in each of the following chapters.

ZACK, SOUTHERN ELECTRICAL SUPPLIES

After a strategic buyer was not identified within the first six months, Zack directed his M&A advisor to pitch SES for sale to a financial buyer. Zack's M&A advisor had previously closed deals with financial buyers who invested in the construction sector.

Within months, multiple private equity firms and family offices were interested in acquiring SES. Several financial buyers delivered letters of intent with respectable offers.

However, initial confidential negotiations showed that none of these buyers were a good fit for Zack. All the financial buyers believed the performance of SES was linked to Zack's leadership, and all would require that Zack remain employed for two or three years. According to Zack's M&A advisor, the private equity firms intended to enhance SES's operating results over a few years, then place it up for sale again.

The prospect of netting a lower sale price and staying employed at SES was contrary to Zack's motivation for selling. The fact that

---

private equity firms could enhance SES's value motivated Zack to work with his M&A advisor to improve his operating efficiencies, inventory management and brand recognition. He redirected his M&A advisor to focus on strategic buyers.

The trial-run of negotiating terms with financial buyers prepared Zack for future negotiations with a strategic buyer. He relied heavily on his M&A advisor to negotiate the deal terms but ultimately decided that none of the offers met his personal needs. He set a new timeline for selling, but realized he was still within his two-year target.

HARRY, ELEGANT CATERING

Under immense pressure to sell, Harry reached out to a former mortgage broker, Mike, who founded and sold a fitness business in San Diego. Mike quickly realized that Harry and Elegant Catering lacked adequate professional support to sell his business.

Mike built his fitness business using a solo CPA who served his family for years. However, before he sold his fitness business Mike engaged a mid-sized local firm, Farley & Co.

Mike referred Harry to Farley & Co in December 2018. The new CPA at Farley & Co. immediately identified several errors in Elegant Catering's past tax returns. Since current QuickBooks were not forthcoming from Elegant Catering's current bookkeeper, Harry hired a new bookkeeping service, one with an automated system and hundreds of virtual bookkeepers working around the country.

Elegant Catering's new bookkeeper had to recreate books for the two prior years and the current year to-date. Harry could not confirm whether all the bank statements, receipts and other accounting records were complete, but his new bookkeeper worked under the caveat that business records were missing.

Farley & Co. referred Harry to a qualified corporate attorney with experience in mergers & acquisitions (an M&A attorney). However, being an attorney himself and being represented by a business broker who would charge a fee equal to 10% of the selling price, Harry didn't believe he should spend money on an M&A attorney.

Meanwhile, his legal bills on Elegant Catering's employment misclassification matter swelled to over $22,000 while the state of California and the IRS were still calculating Elegant Catering's liability for unpaid employment taxes, interest and penalties for misclassification of employees.

Harry's business problems were requiring him to spend more time in Dana Point and generating stress with Nilufer. He wondered if he needed to lower the price further to generate more buyer interest.

Chapter Six:

THE LETTER OF INTENT

Parties to a middle-market M&A transaction should draft, negotiate and sign a letter of intent prior to drafting, negotiating and signing a formal purchase agreement. Drafting a letter of intent (or "LOI") is a prudent step, setting out the major terms in black and white, cutting off futile negotiations, helping a deal move forward and even reducing legal fees. It costs less for attorneys to hammer out the fine print in a 50-page purchase agreement if all the material terms are agreed upon and summarized in a three-page letter of intent.

Consult Your Attorney Before Signing the LOI

An LOI establishes the framework for an extraordinary — possibly life-altering — transaction, but since an LOI is preliminary and non-binding in nature, parties will often draft and sign them without input from legal counsel. Legal advice is more effective and efficient at the earliest stage in negotiations. Good lawyers address the hazards ahead without killing a deal. Any attempts to modify terms based upon tax issues after an LOI is signed can be as difficult as changing the purchase price.

Questions may arise over the legal obligations the parties owe to each other following the execution of an LOI. Disputes over LOIs are not uncommon. A party to an LOI may face uncertainty over whether they bear any binding obligations and may receive varying and inconsistent advice from people who have never read their unique letter.

LOIs run the spectrum. Some are not binding at all (see Appendix B for an example). Some may only create limited obligations like maintaining confidentiality and bearing your own expenses. Others may rise to the level of an enforceable contract with an obligation to negotiate a few remaining issues. Others might contemplate the subsequent execution of a formal agreement but will serve as the final contract if you don't sign a formal agreement.

An LOI can be like a first date or a Vegas wedding. One should be aware of the differences and draft carefully. Courts have upheld certain rules of interpretation for LOIs. The most crucial rule is to determine and honor the intent of parties as reflected in their plain language.

This can be a nuanced exercise. An agreement to agree is not enforceable. However, an agreement to negotiate is enforceable.

Parties usually intend for an LOI to serve as a preliminary reflection of their initial agreement, but not to be bound to such a proposal. If parties expressly state that they don't intend to be bound until final documents are signed, they clearly expect their LOI to be non-binding. However, a mountain of statutes and case law provide ample legal "gray areas" to fuel the fire and prolong a dispute whenever one party feels jilted, especially if a large sum of money is at stake.

The Major Sections of a Letter of Intent

Most letters of intent can be divided into the following sections:
• Identification of the parties and the nature of the transaction.
• The major terms of the deal: Specifics are necessary, including the price and manner by which the price will be paid.
• The buyer will want a binding exclusivity period, so that the seller doesn't continue to promote the business for sale. The buyer will want a long period (60 days) and the seller will want it short (30 days).
• The binding sections, including confidentiality and expenses (each party pays their own advisors).
• The general non-binding language describing which terms are binding and which are not.

Setting Forth the Major Terms of Your Sale

A range of issues will be negotiated and set forth in a letter of intent. The company may be sold through an asset sale, a stock sale or a merger. The LOI will state whether the buyer will pay the purchase price in cash, stock, a promissory note, or some combination thereof. If the consideration is paid through an exchange of publicly traded stock, the LOI will specify whether the buyer provides a fixed or a floating exchange ratio (to accommodate changes in stock prices).

The LOI will reflect whether the parties agree to structure a portion of the purchase price as an "earn-out", contingent upon the future operating results of the acquired business.

If a target company's shareholders will receive stock, and thus become shareholders of the acquirer, agreements limiting resale of the stock such as "lock-up periods" (after an initial public offering) or other trading restrictions might make it difficult for the selling shareholders to realize the maximum value for their stock. If the stock to be received by the target shareholders is that of a privately-owned acquiring company, the LOI should include a provision for due diligence of the acquiring company.

Conversely, shareholders of the target might negotiate for registration rights of the acquiring company stock giving them the ability to sell their shares as part of a future public offering. The target shareholders should consider the pro forma share ownership of the acquirer after closing and their rights to participate in the governance of the acquiring company.

The LOI will specify whether the buyer will retain a portion of the purchase price as a "holdback," how and when the holdback will be paid, and whether such funds will be held in an escrow account. The LOI should confirm whether a portion of the purchase price will be used to retire debt on the target company's books.

The LOI may reflect that the buyer and seller agree upon a purchase price assuming a given "net working capital" balance — current assets minus current liabilities — and that if the actual net working capital on the closing date differs materially from the stipulated balance, the purchase price will be adjusted post-closing.

Although it seems a finer detail and somewhat "legalese," the letter of intent may cover the post-closing indemnification survival periods. In Chapter 11, covering the Purchase Agreement, indemnification and both parties' recourse for losses suffered post-closing will be covered.

Remember that a middle-market M&A transaction is documented in two steps because it is a significant one. Have an attorney review your LOI and make sure your intent is clear on paper. This should be quick, efficient and helpful. Don't find yourself legally married after what you thought was a first date.

Zack, Southern Electrical Supplies

Between November 2018 and March 2019, Zack received several letters of intent from financial buyers. After he pulled out of negotiations with financial buyers, Zack worked with his M&A advisor to target strategic buyers and enhanced the value of SES. Since the financial buyers wanted Zack to remain in full-time management, and they all negotiated a hard bargain, each offered a purchase price which was heavily weighted in the earn-out component.

Zack wanted more allocated to the fixed portion of the price to avoid continuing stress about the operating results of SES. Knowing Zack's needs, his M&A advisor was able to negotiate for a higher fixed price.

Zack's M&A advisor did his own due diligence on the financial standing of each potential buyer and confirmed that none were competitors seeking information about SES. Eventually, in September 2019, a promising buyer was identified.

In October 2019, Zack's M&A advisor negotiated a letter of intent with the electrical division of a major construction conglomerate, RCK Construction. As expected, RCK was interested in an asset sale. RCK wanted Zack to stay employed for two years, but ultimately, they were willing to accept a one-year consulting agreement while RCK relocated a manager to SES's headquarters.

RCK offered a fixed price of $14.5 million and an earn-out over two years with the potential for another $2.5 million. Based on the minimum EBITDA necessary to achieve the earn out, Zack did not expect to receive much, if any, of the earn-out. Zack's M&A advisor was able to renegotiate the price to $15.5 fixed and a $1.2 million earn-out.

SES's M&A attorney provided several comments on the draft LOI, which the buyer accepted into the final version. The deal terms were non-binding, but after much negotiation, the October 12, 2019 letter of intent was a firm foundation for completing the sale.

Harry, Elegant Catering

Harry's employee misclassification matter dragged out for over 10 months, while agents audited his business records and spoke to his staff. Through May 2019, two potential buyers were prescreened by Harry's broker and determined to be qualified buyers. After signing non-disclosure agreements, both buyers were provided the two most recent tax returns of Elegant Catering, returns for 2014 and 2015.

Both buyers expressed grave concern over the lack of current financial statements to support the asking price, uncertainty about Elegant Catering's current operating results and financial condition and unknown tax problems. One buyer, Mac, who was familiar with Elegant Catering's dominance at Bayside Views, made a lowball offer of $1 million in a non-binding letter of intent, and Harry signed it. Immediately, Mac's M&A attorney delivered a standard but extensive due diligence request list. Harry's broker was unable to deliver documents responsive to most of the requests.

During one meeting, Harry inadvertently mentioned the IRS employee misclassification matter to Mac. Mac's attorney demanded all records related to the employee misclassification matter. One day after these documents were delivered to Mac's attorney, Mac called to inform Harry that the deal was off. No purchase agreement was ever drafted for Mac's proposed acquisition.

Chapter Seven:

ACCOUNTING

FINANCIAL AND TAX ACCOUNTING

Accounting is the process of capturing and reporting the financial condition and operating results of a business. Accounting includes financial reporting, tax accounting and cost accounting. Businesses have internal accounting staff and outside professional accountants.

Tax accounting is driven by the rules set forth in the Internal Revenue Code and the rulings and regulations adopted and enforced by the IRS, along with analogous laws and regulations in each of the 50 states. The end-result of tax accounting is a tax return which sets forth taxable income and thus "income tax expense". As with all other expenses, business owners seek to minimize income taxes. This goal of lowering tax expense requires lower taxable income.

Financial accounting is based upon standards written by the Financial Accounting Standards Board (FASB). Businesses follow the FASB's financial accounting standards in varying degrees. Businesses report their operating results and financial condition to investors pursuant to financial accounting rules. Stock prices are based upon financial accounting, whether through earnings announced on CNBC, an appraiser who values a business or the prospective buyer who scrutinizes your financial statements.

Financial reporting seeks higher net income to maximize the value of the business, and tax accounting generally seeks lower taxable income to minimize income expense. Thus, the rub.

CPA FIRMS

Businesses use outside accounting professionals to support their internal accounting staff. A Certified Public Accountant should prepare the tax returns for a business. If you cannot afford a CPA, an Enrolled Agent should prepare the tax returns. Any business tax returns which are not prepared by a tax professional will be met with skepticism by prospective buyers, bankers, lawyers, accountants, and anyone else who may review them.

A middle-market business may also use an independent CPA firm to attest to its financial statements. From highest to lowest, the level of attestation services ranges from an audit, a review, a compilation and, lastly, preparation services. Publicly traded companies must have audited financial statements. Often banks or investors will require a business to prepare audited financial statements, or possibly to have a review of their financials. Certain private securities offerings will require the preparation of audited financial statements.

The lack of financial integrity is one of the most common hurdles encountered during the sale process. In addition, the best way to demonstrate the sustainability of your company's earnings is to have its historical financial statements audited by an independent, certified public accounting firm. An audit demonstrates to the potential buyers that the historical information can be relied upon when making judgments about buying the company based on historical cash flows. It is very important to have your CPA review your current financial statements and practices so that any financial irregularities or inadequacies are immediately exposed and corrected.[10]

ACCOUNTING INFORMATION SYSTEMS AND STAFF

Many businesses are stingy with their internal accounting staff. Many companies should employ a qualified chief financial officer but instead employ someone qualified to be a controller. Those who need a controller might hire someone qualified to work as an accounting manager. Those needing an accounting manager may use an outside bookkeeper.

Business owners may justify these savings believing better accounting is an unnecessary expense. When it comes time to sell a business, these "savings" may cause a lower sales price. These "savings" may even torpedo a sale.

If you are happy with your accumulated savings on accounting expenses, it's wise to invest some of that money into a thorough review and clean-up of your books before trying to sell.

Companies maintain an accounting system, which may be a staff of hundreds of accountants and supercomputers or a business owner with a stack of invoices in a shoebox. The only business owner who should do their own bookkeeping is one who makes a living as a bookkeeper. A business should strive to use the best qualified CPA along with the most appropriate accounting staff and accounting system.

When signing a purchase agreement of a middle-market business, the owner will vouch for the accuracy of the business's financial statements and bear risk of their misstatement. As with any important business function, an owner must have the proper accounting team and oversee their work well enough to speak intelligently on the subject.

For a small business, its tax return may be the most reliable accounting report that the business prepares. The small business will also provide the buyer with financial statements, but the tax returns will be used to judge the reliability of the financial statements. A buyer and appraiser will consider financial statements, tax returns, and other accounting reports.

All financial information will be subjected to scrutiny through the due diligence process. Buyers will review all the financial information a business can provide, such as sales reports, and details on accounts receivable and accounts payable. A business owner should invest in a system to provide reliable financial information while reporting their operating results and financial condition in the most favorable light possible. This is an investment that can increase the sales price.

RESTATEMENT OF FINANCIAL STATEMENTS

Your financial statements may need to be restated — substantially — as you prepare for the sale and complete a valuation of your business. Expenses which reflect the owner's high degree of personal control over the company's finances may require adjustments which either increase or decrease income and may have a material impact on the valuation of the business. One-time, non-recurring or unusual expenses might be included in adjusted income. This topic will be covered in Chapter 8 on Valuation.

ACCOUNTING FOR MERGERS & ACQUISITIONS

Financial Accounting

Financial accounting for the acquisition of a middle-market business may be much more complicated for the buyer, particularly if your company is acquired by a strategic buyer — and especially if the buyer is a publicly traded company. The FASB has eliminated the old practice of "pooling accounting" where an acquirer could add the assets and liabilities of your business to its own balance sheet at book value (the balances recorded on the balance sheet).

Today, all acquisitions must implement "purchase accounting" where the assets and liabilities of the acquired business are booked at their "fair value"—their estimated market value. Estimation of fair value may present challenges for the acquiring company, particularly with assets which have never been recorded on your books before like internally developed intangible assets and intellectual property. The balance of the purchase price, over and above the net fair value of the acquired assets and liabilities, is recorded on the books of the acquiring company as "goodwill" —the intangible value of an operating business in excess of the aggregate value of its individual assets and liabilities.

Tax Accounting

In an asset sale, the buyer and seller must agree upon the allocation of the purchase price among the assets of the acquired business. The buyer will want to allocate more of the purchase price to assets which can be quickly depreciated (like equipment) or expensed in the current year (like inventory) in order to reduce tax liabilities as soon as possible. As a seller, you want to minimize the allocation of the purchase price to assets which will lead to ordinary income such as inventory and accounts receivable.

Allocation of the purchase price to the following assets normally produces long-term capital gain and thus benefits the seller:
- Land
- Buildings (which were not depreciated under accelerated rules)
- Intellectual property (patents, trademarks, copyrights and other IP)
- Goodwill

Allocation of the purchase price to the following assets may cause the seller to recognize ordinary income:
- Accounts Receivable
- Buildings (if depreciated under accelerated rules)
- Equipment (if depreciated under accelerated rules)
- Furniture and fixtures (if depreciated under accelerated rules)
- Non-compete agreement

As the seller, you will try to allocate the maximum amount of the sales price to goodwill to obtain long-term capital gains treatment on this balance. Valuable goodwill that is based on your professional skills and business relationships can be treated as "personal goodwill" and taxed as capital gains. Goodwill is amortized by the buyer over a longer period. Thus, the buyer will seek to allocate more of the price to other assets.

The amount attributed to goodwill must be reasonable in relation to the purchase price. According to Greg McGahan, CPA, a partner at PricewaterhouseCoopers, "It's the residual, but accountants should be able to validate it. If 40% of the purchase price is allocated to goodwill, does that make sense based on the deal or value drivers? Things like future customers, platform, and company-specific synergies all go to goodwill."[11]

The buyer's and seller's accountants should be involved early in the sale process in order to contribute to the process. According to Aaron Saito, CPA, Capital Accounting controller at Intel Corp., it is crucial to understand the accounting ramifications up front. "Once the ink is dry on the contract, you don't have options," Saito said.[12]

Tax-Free Exchanges

A transaction where you accept more than 50% of the consideration in stock of the acquiring company may be a tax-free exchange, or partially tax-free. A cash-free, all-stock merger generally does not trigger a taxable event. A limited liability company may not participate in a tax-free exchange, making an S corporation more beneficial.

Summary

Accounting is probably not the glamorous aspect of business which attracted you to become an entrepreneur. CPAs are not known for hosting the best happy hours. However, your accounting should be subjected to scrutiny and analysis by you and your M&A Team to ensure your financial statements and accounting records help facilitate a sale for top dollar, instead of scaring away a buyer.

Zack, Southern Electrical Supplies

Ella, her controller and accounting managers maintained reliable books and records for SES using NetSuite ERP. Having several members among its accounting staff, SES was able to implement proper internal controls, ensuring that transactions were properly authorized, custody of assets was segregated from record-keeping and reconciliations were prepared and independently reviewed.

In 1991, Zack engaged Sells & Staff to prepare state and federal income tax returns and provide periodic assistance with other taxes, such as property and sales taxes. SES used an outside payroll service, with Ella reviewing monthly and annual payroll reports.

SES did not prepare GAAP-based financial statements until 2017 when Zack's M&A advisor recommended that SES prepare GAAP financials and have them reviewed. Ella worked with her accounting staff to prepare the GAAP-based financial statements, although they lacked footnotes.

Sells & Staff sent two staff members to SES's office to review their financial statements. Sells & Staff proposed, and SES recorded, several adjustments to SES's financial statements. Sells & Staff issued a review opinion which noted the deviation from GAAP due to the omission of footnotes.

SES's bank relied upon the reviewed financial statements and its recent tax returns to open SES's line of credit. In 2018, private equity firms and family offices analyzed SES's GAAP financial statements.

When private equity firms were considering an acquisition of SES, their accountants made suggestions about how SES could be restructured with multiple LLCs to generate more tax efficient flow-through of SES's profits. The private equity firms suggested that SES generate pro forma financial statements and instruct their attorneys to craft a new corporate structure.

Zack relied upon the advice of his M&A advisor, corporate attorney and CPA to stand firm with his reliable financial statements and tax returns. If a deal was reached with a private equity firm, SES could work with the buyer to make any necessary corporate reorganization and accounting changes. The financials of SES were sufficiently reliable for buyers to run their own pro forma analyses.

In 2019, RCK analyzed SES's financial statements before confirming a valuation and delivering its letter of intent. RCK's own accounting staff prepared its own pro forma consolidated financial statements during their due diligence and applications for mezzanine financing.

Harry, Elegant Catering

Harry paid Farley and Co. and his new bookkeeper a combined total of $35,000 to recreate his books for the past two years and 10 months, file amended tax returns for 2014 and 2015 and file returns for 2016 through 2018. Helen mistakenly filed partnership tax returns for 2014 and 2015, even though Harry bought out Skip's interest in Elegant Catering in 2014, which terminated the partnership.

With only one owner, Elegant Catering's LLC was now a "disregarded entity" for tax purposes and all the income and expenses of Elegant Catering should have been filed on Harry's personal tax return. The amended and most recent tax returns were filed in May 2019, just as Mac was terminating his interest in buying Elegant Catering.

Harry borrowed $20,000 from Nilufer to help pay the $35,000 cost of accounting. He promised to pay her back when the sale closed.

Chapter Eight:

VALUATION

SUPPORT YOUR ASKING PRICE

A small business which is marketed for sale with an arbitrary and high asking price will rarely attract buyers' interest and is not likely to sell for anything close to this original arbitrary sum. When marketing or listing your business for sale you should have a defensible estimate of what your business is worth.

Small businesses, commonly sold through business brokers, must undertake more advance valuation efforts than middle-market companies. Larger middle-market companies are bought and sold by more financially savvy buyers and sellers, and thus the parties will rely more upon the market to set the selling price. Defensible calculations of value help all sellers in their negotiations.

If you haven't previously issued stock to sophisticated investors who assigned a valuation to your company through their investment, this might be the first time you have ever conducted a meaningful exercise to determine what your business is worth. So, keep an open mind and try to determine the most defensible value for your business.

Valuation is subject to various professional norms and several standard methods of valuing a business. The most appropriate method to value your business depends upon the nature of your business.

Do you have a long history of profitable operations? Do you own valuable fixed assets which cost a significant sum to accumulate? Have you developed unique technology or a valuable brand which will lead to future profits? Is your business comparable to any publicly traded companies or recently acquired businesses? All these factors will weigh into the choice of the most appropriate valuation method.

Whether you will need a formal "appraisal" from an independent business valuation firm, something short of an appraisal (such as a professional "calculation") or simply assistance estimating your value from an M&A advisor or business broker, you need something in writing which supports the price you expect to be paid. If you can't support your asking price in writing, don't expect to receive your asking price.

Often, you should obtain an appraisal of your business from a qualified appraiser, using several of the standard valuation methods and setting forth the valuation factors related to your business. Get the appraisal well in advance of the sale. Such an appraisal might cost from $3,000 to $10,000. You can find a qualified appraiser through referrals from other members of your M&A Team.

It is important that you know what your business is currently worth and understand the primary methods of valuation and factors taken into consideration.

Many business professionals will volunteer their opinion, verbally, about the value of your business, but many will avoid putting pen to paper with their own name attached to a valuation. Your CPA or attorney won't want exposure to liability for providing services outside of their qualifications or to confuse their professional role.

An appraisal from a top-tier firm may cost between $10,000 to $20,000, or even more, which may seem like a dear price for a report and supporting data generated over a few weeks. However, this investment is highly likely to pay off multifold in your final sale proceeds.   In the absence of defensible support, an arbitrarily priced business may sit on the market for years.

Valuation Methods

There are a number of common valuation methods:

- EBITDA method
- Adjusted Cash Flows/Seller's Discretionary Earnings
- Discounted cash flows
- Comparable companies
- Asset accumulation method
- Acquisition debt value
- Liquidation value
- Rule of thumb formulas

For purposes of this book, we will focus on the EBITDA method; however, all these approaches will be discussed below. The EBITDA method is the most commonly used to value middle-market businesses. Adjusted Cash Flows/Seller's Discretionary Earnings is the method most often used for Main Street businesses.

The proper choice of method may depend on the size and industry of your business:

A number of businesses are valued by buyers based upon accounting earnings or income. Indeed, one of the most common methods of valuation is the so-called EBITDA method. This involves the determination of your accounting earnings before interest, taxes, depreciation, and amortization (EBITDA), and multiplication of the EBITDA by the relevant multiplier to obtain a business valuation.[13]

The EBITDA Method

This summary illustrates the steps in the valuation of your company using the EBITDA method:

- Calculating EBITDA
- Adjusting EBITDA
- Selecting the earnings period(s)
- Choosing among EBITDA multipliers

EBITDA

Earnings Before Interest Taxes Depreciation and Amortization is the most common measure of profitability used to determine the value of a middle-market business (see Table 8.1). EBITDA is similar to other measures of profitability, but it can be especially useful for comparing companies with different capital structures, debt and tax attributes.

Adding back depreciation and amortization to net income eliminates expenses which don't cost cash, and thereby reflecting the cash earnings generated by the business. Interest and taxes are added back to better compare the operating profitability of a company in an "apples to apples" manner.

DESCRIPTION	TAXABLE ENTITY	PASS-THROUGH ENTITY
Revenue	$10,000,000	$10,000,000
Cost of sales	6,000,000	6,000,000
Gross profit	4,000,000	4,000,000
Selling, General & Admin. Exp.	2,200,000	2,200,000
Income before taxes	1,800,000	1,800,000
Income taxes	630,000	
EBITDA Calculation:		
Net Income	$1,170,000	$1,800,000
Interest expense	200,000	200,000
Income taxes	630,000	
Depreciation expense	150,000	150,000
Amortization expenses	20,000	20,000
EBITDA	$2,170,000	$2,170,000

Table 8.1

Adjusting EBITDA

As discussed in Chapter 7, the financial statements of a small business are often adjusted to account for a variety of issues.

> Your EBITDA is then adjusted to remove expenses and revenue that will no longer be carried forward into the new business. These adjustments can be quite substantial for a closely held family business.

> Most closely held businesses are operated to minimize income taxes. As a result, excessive compensation and perquisites may be provided to the owner and his family in order to reduce taxes. The excessive compensation and perquisites are really forms of disguised dividends.[14]

As part of the income statement adjustment process, some business owners must address issues related to income tax avoidance. All the various adjustments may cause increases or decreases to EBITDA, and they may have a material — usually positive — impact on the valuation of the business:

- The owner's personal expenses paid by the business, such as computers, cell phones, travel and meals.
- Vehicle expenses for the owner and family members.
- Excessive compensation to the owners and their family.
- Below-market compensation to the owners.
- Country club memberships or similar expenses not necessary to the business.

- Professional sports tickets.
- Tuition for family members.
- Vacations or personal travel expenses.
- Excessive insurance benefits for the owners and their family, including health, life, and liability.
- Office or warehouse rent paid to an owner that is in excess of, or below, market value rent.
- Bonuses or other perks that are above-market.
- Maintenance, repairs, remodeling or insurance for the owner's personal residence.
- Legal fees for personal legal matters.

Salaries paid to owners and their family members usually trigger the need for adjustment, as demonstrated by the following examples:

> The owner/manager of Company A draws no salary from the company. His market salary would be $200,000 per year, or $250,000 grossed up with all payroll and social security taxes. If an investor were to buy this business, the former owner/manager would presumably not be prepared to stay and work for free indefinitely; nor would a replacement be willing to work for free. Presumably the new managers would ask for a market salary. Hence EBITDA and ... would be [reduced] by $250,000.[15]

Salary adjustments can work in the opposite way, increasing the adjusted EBITDA of a business:

The son of the owner/manager of Company B is 17 years old and is working part-time for Company B, drawing a salary of $100,000 (fully grossed up). The son is not producing anything of value for Company B, nor would the investor wish to continue with the son on the payroll. In this case, EBITDA and EBIT would be increased by $100,000.[16]

Certain expenses are likely to be incurred once or will be substantially lower in future periods. Below are examples of nonrecurring or extraordinary expenses that might be accounted for in the adjusted EBITDA:

- Extraordinary capital expenditures.
- Opening a new location or facility.
- Costs of the Exit Plan: M&A legal expenses, audit, appraisal or consulting fees preparing for the sale, redemption of minority owners.
- Legal costs of corporate restructuring or reorganization.
- Litigation expenses.
- Computer and information system upgrades.
- Marketing, branding, public relations or research costs.
- Leases or fixed assets that were expensed instead of being properly capitalized.
- Legal and accounting fees to implement an Employee Stock Option Plan or a similar plan.

The Appropriate Valuation Periods

Your valuation team will discuss the appropriate income periods for the adjusted EBITDA calculations. There are several options:

- Trailing 12-month period
- Trailing 24-month period
- Trailing 36-month period
- Weighted three-year period

After determining the proper periods for inclusion, a 12-month average of EBITDA is calculated and multiplied by the chosen multiplier. Alternatively, a weighted average favoring the most recent periods is calculated and multiplied by the chosen multiplier.

The Appropriate Multiplier for Your Business

Once adjusted, EBITDA needs to be multiplied by a factor chosen from a certain range of numbers that are called "multipliers." The multipliers are necessary to the complete the valuation of your business.

The adjusted EBITDA is then multiplied by a multiplier to obtain an overall valuation for the business (also called "enterprise value"). The multiplier typically ranges from 4 to 6 times adjusted EBITDA, particularly for financial buyers. However, the multiplier has gone below 4 and substantially above 6, depending upon whether it is a buyer's market or a seller's market for the sale of businesses. A multiplier above 6 is more typical for strategic rather than financial buyers.

Multipliers of 20 or more are not unheard of for strategic buyers of companies with strong market niches.

The multipliers are derived from comparable company valuations, including the multipliers applicable to public companies in the same industry. For example, if a public company in your industry has a total market valuation (based on its stock price) of 10 times its EBITDA, this multiplier could be the starting point in determining the appropriate multiplier.

This multiplier would then be discounted by the fact that your company was smaller and has less market dominance.

Many business owners incorrectly assume that the multipliers applicable to larger companies in the industry apply to their smaller company. The multipliers for less dominant companies in an industry are significantly smaller than for dominant companies.[17]

Several business valuation resources (such as the Business Reference Guide and PeerComps) provide industry data on multipliers based on actual sales of other businesses. These resources also provide multipliers used for other methods, particularly the Adjusted Cash Flows/Seller's Discretionary Earnings Method. The appropriate multiplier often reflects the nature of the buyer and the sale transaction:

Transaction	Multiple
Strategic Buyer	8-10x
Private Equity (Financial Buyer)	6-8x
Management Buyout (MBO)	5-7x
ESOP	5-6x

18

After selecting the EBITDA method, accounting to determine EBITDA for your business, adjusting EBITDA for each of the expenses that will be altered after the business is sold, determining the appropriate historical period of EBITDA to use and the appropriate multiplier, your valuation professional can provide a defensible valuation of your business.

Valuation Advice from a Financial Advisor

Your financial advisor often has a unique market perspective to judge the selling price. Kirk Michie of AB Bernstein offers the following advice regarding valuations:

Am I getting fair value for my business? The marketplace drives the answer to this question. It has nothing to do with the seller's goals or preferences. To determine fair value, especially in an active M&A environment, speaking to a business broker (for businesses with less than $10 million of enterprise value) or investment banker (for business in excess of $10 million of enterprise value) who has been active in that sector will provide a reasonable range of valuation parameters.

Most companies sell at either a multiple of EBITDA or revenue, with EBITDA being more common for most mature businesses.

For example, a company with $20 million of revenue, and $2 million of EBITDA, in a sector that trades at 6x to 8x EBITDA is worth $12 million to $16 million. For faster growing companies, especially in the technology sector, where growth or intellectual property is more important to buyers than profitability, businesses sell for multiple of revenue.

For example, an attractive software company with the same financial information as the prior example might sell for 2x or 3x revenue, or $40 million to $60 million. The key driver is how much demand there is on the part of buyers (strategic or financial), how they plan to integrate the business into their company or portfolio, and how they can best optimize (cross-selling, leveraged distribution, etc.) the company being acquired.

Multiples ebb and flow with deal activity (where more activity in the markets will boost higher multiples), interest rates (where lower rates generate more activity), and demand (more buyers, and more aggressive buyers generate higher multiples).[19]

Other Valuation Methods

Your business should be valued using multiple methods to determine the most appropriate method and find the highest defensible valuation:

Adjusted Cash Flows/Seller's Discretionary Earnings

This method is the commonly used to appraise small businesses, particularly those sold through a business broker. The process works much like the adjusted EBITDA method where non-cash expenses are added back to net income. In addition, all the owner's compensation and personal benefits are added back to net income to reflect the total cash benefit a business owner derives from operating their business.

The Adjusted Cash Flows (also known as Seller's Discretionary Earnings or Owner's Discretionary Cash Flows) are then multiplied by a factor based on comparable sales of similarly sized businesses in the same industry. The multiplier is typically much lower than a multiple used for EBITDA, but the resulting value is a good indicator of how much a bank will lend for the acquisition of such an owner-operated business.

Discounted Cash Flows

This method projects cash flows from business operations and discounts them back to their present value based on time and risk factors. Starting with revenue, gross margins and net operating profits, adjustments are then made to add back non-cash expenses such as depreciation and amortization as well to deduct cash outflows for capital expenditures.

These balances are projected out for a given period, typically five or 10 years and discounted back to their present value. A terminal or residual value may be calculated by capitalizing the final year's projected cash flows as if it were an annuity or applying a multiplier to the final year's cash flow. After calculating the total value of the business enterprise, debt is subtracted to determine the value of equity ownership.

Comparable Companies

If your middle-market business is comparable to publicly traded companies, you may use a public company as a benchmark for valuing your company. You would look to the total market capitalization of a publicly traded company (the market price of its stock multiplied by the number of issued and outstanding shares) and adjust to scale to the size of your business (using objective criteria, such as sales, EBITDA, net income or book value—the net value of the company based on its balance sheet).

Note that the total market capitalization of a publicly traded company will not include a "control premium" which is being sold to the buyer of your business. However, since your company is privately owned, your equity is subject to a "liquidity discount" since the shares cannot be easily resold to a third party.

Asset Accumulation Method

Often used as a minimum valuation, this approach adds the going concern value of each of the assets used in the business. The going concern value of each asset could be calculated based upon the replacement cost, an income approach or market approach. The most subjective and disputed asset included within this method is the value of goodwill and other intangible assets.

Acquisition Debt Value

Acquisition debt value is another measure of the minimum value of a business. This measures the maximum amount of debt that can be serviced using the excess cash flow generated by the business. If $200,000 of EBITDA would provide enough cash to service $2.5 million of debt with a market rate bank loan, then $2.5 million would be a minimum valuation of the business. Acquisition debt value is not uncommon with sales of small businesses requiring bank financing because banks tend to be conservative when lending for such acquisitions.

Liquidation Value

If a business is not generating positive cash flows and not projected to generate positive cash flows, the proceeds from an orderly liquidation may be used as a minimum valuation.

Rule-of-Thumb Formulas

While often simple and usually detached from financial accounting, rule-of-thumb formulas can be useful if they are broadly accepted within your industry. For example, valuation of vending machine businesses may be based on the number of locations, cable TV businesses on the number of subscribers and hospice care operations based on the number of patients under care. Rule-of-thumb formulas are used with smaller businesses.

Ultimately, Negotiations

The final selling price of your business will reflect negotiations with the buyer, but your negotiating position will be bolstered by a credible valuation based on solid accounting. Often the parties can reach a creative compromise, including the use of an earn-out.

For example, if your business would typically sell for four to eight times EBITDA, a seller might offer you four times EBITDA. You could counter at eight times EBITDA. The buyer might claim they have a limit of five times EBITDA. You might agree to a fixed price at five times EBITDA along with an earn-out giving you the potential to earn up to an additional three times EBITDA. Creativity and compromise can lead to the best outcome for both parties to the sale.

Zack, Southern Electrical Supplies

Based on the earnings and consistent profitability of SES, Zack's M&A advisor valued the business using the EBITDA method. Ella and SES's M&A advisor worked together to determine SES's adjusted EBITDA. All interest, taxes and non-cash expenses were added back to net income. SES's CPA reviewed the EBITDA calculation and verbally confirmed it was correct, although EBITDA is not reflected on SES's GAAP financials or its tax returns.

Since the founding of SES, Zack consistently took a low salary and paid the maximum distributions to himself to save on payroll taxes. Thus, SES EBITDA was adjusted downward to reflect the market salary a CEO would demand to manage SES.

However, Zack also expensed and deducted all costs associated with his wife's vehicle, which was not used in SES's operations. His family cell phones were all included on a single plan which was expensed and deducted by SES. Zack's membership at the Faircrest Country Club was not truly a source of business marketing. All these costs were added back to determine adjusted EBITDA.

SES was similar to other middle-market wholesalers in construction-related businesses. SES's M&A advisor reviewed current industry data of similar acquisitions by strategic buyers in electrical sales wholesaling and determined that businesses generating EBITDA like SES, typically sell for a multiple of six to seven. Private equity firms consistently offered multiples of five to 5.5.

With reliable reviewed financial statements, accurate calculations of and adjustments to EBITDA, and an appropriate multiplier, SES's average EBITDA over the past three years was multiplied by 6.5 to determine an enterprise value of $16.3 million. The current balance on SES's line of credit was subtracted to reach a final equity value of $16.1 million.

Valuation of SES using the adjusted cash flows method generated a comparable value to the EBITDA method, supporting the EBITDA-based valuation. The valuation based on adjusted cash flows was $15.7 million which was included in the brochure used to generate investor interest. Valuations using alternative methods, such as asset accumulation and debt service, were much lower than an EBITDA method, and inappropriate for a company with high and consistent earnings like SES.

Harry, Elegant Catering

Elegant Catering was initially listed for sale at $2.5 million, a sum which Harry believed would last him through his retirement. The asking price was then lowered to $2 million. Elegant Catering's tax returns (and thus any reliable financial statements) were unavailable until May 2019. After Elegant Catering's operating results were reflected on tax returns through 2018, Harry's business broker was able to prepare a valuation of Elegant Catering.

Harry's business broker prepared a standard small business valuation based upon adjusted cash flows (seller's discretionary earnings). Harry's broker had access to industry data to review comparable sales data and multiples.

Harry's salary was added back to net income. In addition, Harry charged a long list of personal expenses to Elegant Catering's business. This included all the rent and utilities for his apartment, his cell phone, and his trips to visit Nilufer in New York — trips which bore no relationship to Elegant Catering's business operations. These personal costs were added back to income.

Harry's broker also added back non-cash expenses and interest expense charged against Elegant Catering's taxable income. After adding back Harry's compensation and personal expenses, Elegant Catering's interest expense and non-cash expenses, Harry's broker determined the "adjusted cash flows" or "seller's discretionary earnings" for Elegant Catering's past three years of operations.

Based on an average adjusted cash flow derived from the business over 2016 through 2018 of $370,000 and using a multiple of 2.8 (based on sales of comparable businesses) the value of Elegant Catering was estimated to be $1,036,000, rounded to $1,000,000.

With financial data in hand showing the business was not worth anything close to $2 million, and desperate to find a buyer, Harry lowered the asking price of Elegant Catering to $1 million. Harry's broker explained that such a dramatic price reduction would raise eyebrows with potential buyers, but they should attribute the reduction to stale accounting data — not changes in the operations of the business.

Chapter Nine:

BOOSTING THE VALUE OF YOUR BUSINESS

One of the biggest advantages of early planning is that you will have time to boost the value of your business. You can build upon your competitive strengths and minimize your competitive weakness.

> You can increase the value of your business if you understand how buyers are likely to value it.[20]

You should seek ways to enhance the value of your business before selling it. These value-building actions fall into two broad categories:
- Altering your business methods or operations so that current or future operations generate higher profits and adequately protect your assets, and
- Modifying your accounting methods to boost your operating results and financial condition.

Profitability drives value:

> For each $1 that you increase your EBITDA during the valuation year, you should arguably receive an additional $4 to $6 in sale price.[21]

> There are measures you can take to increase the value of your business when a sale is imminent—within 18 months or so. There are ways to increase your payday, by millions of dollars in many cases. Just as importantly, there are methods of transforming a marginal business into a saleable one.[22]

Actions to Boost Value

Obviously, you can do more to build value the earlier you start preparing for your exit. Beginning with the first category of value-enhancing actions, your exit strategy process will focus on four items:

- Increasing sales and diversification of sales.
- Improving profit margins.
- Enhancing operating processes and efficiencies.
- Branding and marketing.

Positive Factors	Negative Factors
Lasting, positive customer relationships.	Poor customer relationships and high turnover.
Recognized and respected brand.	Commodity or business with poor reputation.
Broad customer base with no single customer accounting for more than five percent of revenue.	Customer concentration, particularly with a single customer accounting for over 15% of revenue.
Strong, experienced and qualified management team.	A weak management team or poor relationships among management.
Positive employee retention and relations.	High employee turnover and poor relations.
Consistent revenue and earnings trends.	Erratic revenue and earnings trends.
Property, plant and equipment maintained in good condition.	Property, plant and equipment has been neglected, obsolete or requires major repairs.
Legal protection of intellectual property in registration and IP agreements.	Lack of legally protected intellectual property and poor IP documentation.

Table 9.1 Factors Impacting Your Value

In addition, you should develop a strategy to minimize your own distractions from the sale so that the sale process doesn't cause your earnings to suffer.

Sales Force

As a business owner, you are focused on growing your revenue. However, you should build a sales force which can function after you leave. You do not want your potential buyer to conclude: "[A]s a buyer we would not be buying a fully functioning business as was represented. Really, we are buying [Mr. Entrepreneur's] personal book of business (much like a sales rep's book of business)."

Your buyer wants to see that you have a product or service—with a brand—that your sales force can successfully sell. A buyer will be leery of acquiring a business that is dependent upon one superstar salesperson.

Your objective is to hire salespeople who can sell your products and services while you are able to devote your time and energy to managing the company and building value.

Branding

Branding your business is the complement to increasing and diversifying sales. A thorough review of your company's brand, especially as compared to your competition, would be a worthy investment of your time and should be done periodically regardless of whether you are selling or not. Although it may seem like too much to add to your plate, you might consider hiring a marketing firm with a good reputation for brand development and solutions. Your branding will impact future sales to customers and the sale of your business to a buyer.

Just like you would never market your products or services without an understanding of what your customers want, the same applies to the sale of your business. For you to receive the maximum value, you need to understand what they want.

Your buyer wants to acquire a company with a respected brand. It may take years to realize the value of successful branding through future profits. However, innovative enhancement of your branding strategy should be apparent to your buyer and boost the sales price of your business.

Operating Results

Focus on long-term investments in your key operating functions to generate higher future profits.

Owners who focus on maximizing their company's gross margins often unlock substantial value. By definition, this means maximizing [on] cost of goods sold. The best investment most owners can make is upgrading the company's purchasing function. Professional materials management pays for itself many times over and helps create market value. Companies can benefit greatly from installing cutting-edge inventory management and other throughput management systems.[23]

Minimize Distractions During the Sale

Below are some ideas to assist you in avoiding distractions arising from the negotiation, technical agreements, due diligence and inevitable stress, and to move forward in closing the transaction:

- Delegate the maximum number of tasks to the appropriate member of your M&A Team.
- Hold the members of your M&A Team accountable for their tasks.
- Replace unreliable members of your M&A Team (if you're in the early stages of the sale process).
- Continue to manage your business as if the sale will not close.
- Continue to manage your business up to the closing day.

Manage your M&A Team and keep the sale process moving forward. Expect more than a few bumps on the road. Focus on the vision and direction of your business and continue to require the best from your management team.

Accounting Methods

If you start planning well in advance of a sale and employ the services of the right accounting professionals, you can adopt accounting methods which will reflect higher operating margins. As you get closer to the sales process, accountants can help you prepare restated (historical pro forma) financial statements and pro forma financial statements reflecting future profits using appropriate favorable accounting methods.

The appropriate accounting methods depend upon your industry. Generally Accepted Accounting Principles (GAAP) often provide multiple alternative accounting methods, all being acceptable. Your goal is to consistently apply acceptable methods which boost your earnings.

Zack, Southern Electrical Supplies

SES's inventory management software was outdated, causing it to hold too much inventory and incur excessive losses on obsolete inventory. With minimal borrowing to supplement its current cash balances, SES implemented a new logistics management software to integrate with multiple carriers.

Zack also retained the services of FlameStick to provide a fixed fee branding project and enhance SES's image and name-recognition. SES had not invested any time or resources into public relations or branding since 2001, leaving the company with a stale brand in the marketplace.

These enhancements were implemented after the negotiations with financial buyers. Although these costs reduced earnings over the short-term, they demonstrated a long-term vision for the success of SES, not an owner who was so focused on selling that he lost interest in managing the business.

It would be impossible to attribute the increase in the price (between offers received from financial buyers and RCK's final price) solely to these investments, but Zack was confident they helped attract RCK and cause them to "fall in love" with SES.

Harry, Elegant Catering

Harry and Nilufer agreed to take time off from their relationship. The burdens on Harry of managing and selling a business along with Nil's demanding career made for an impossible long-distance relationship. Harry promised to sell Elegant Catering quickly, repay Nil's loan and return to New York. Nil wasn't overly concerned about $20,000, so much as she disapproved of Harry's irresponsible business and financial mismanagement.

As a merchant banker, Nil had participated in debt restructuring and operating turnarounds for major companies in all industries all over the globe. Although Elegant Catering was below the scale of operations Nil usually restructured, she believed Harry's neglect had led to a complacent workforce and a concentrated customer base.

Harry took the bold step of firing his two least reliable banquet captains, promoting a promising young server to captain and hiring a new banquet server from a competitor (Indulge) who dominated the other event properties in Dana Point. Two cooks were also hired from Indulge to reduce the workload on Elegant Catering's kitchen staff.

Indulge was profitable, well capitalized and growing, expanding its operations throughout Orange County.

Harry was able to land major catering contracts at two additional properties. Harry reinvested profits into a marketing program with a local PR firm to generate more weddings and corporate events.

Soon thereafter, the three owners of Indulge invited Harry out for dinner at the Ritz Carlton. Harry expected that Indulge may be interested in buying Elegant Catering, so he brought a non-disclosure agreement to the dinner. After discussing Elegant Catering's current customer base, growth, current staff and marketing efforts, Indulge made a verbal offer of $1.2 million.

On the following day, February 3, 2020, Indulge delivered a non-binding letter of intent reflecting a fixed price of $1 million and an earn-out of $200,000. Harry's broker was able to negotiate the price to $1.1 million fixed and $100,000 through an earn-out based on Revenue over the 12 months after closing. Since Indulge already operated in Dana Point, the buyers only asked for Harry to stay employed for 30 days after the closing.

Chapter Ten:

FINANCING THE SALE

Asset Sale or Stock Sale

The most common transaction structure used for the sale of a small or middle-market company is a sale of all the assets used in the business. However, as a seller, you may benefit by selling your stock and realizing more capital gains.

In either case the buyer must finance the transaction in roughly the same manner. In an asset sale, the purchase price will be delivered to the company (your corporation). With a stock sale, the purchase price will be paid to the owners of the company.

In most middle-market transactions, the purchase price is paid with some combination of cash at closing, deferred payments of cash, and possibly seller financing (where you accept a promissory note from the buyer). Some of these asset sales or stock sale transactions include payment of a portion of the purchase price in the form of stock (where the buyer issues or exchanges shares of its own stock to the seller).

Third Party Financing

Financing a portion of the purchase price through a third-party lender is a customary practice. Your buyer may be able to obtain a conventional loan from a bank or a loan which is partially guaranteed the U.S. Small Business Administration ("SBA").

Either loan would be secured with a first-priority lien against the assets of the business. Thus, any seller financing would be subordinated to the bank loan (i.e., you would hold a second-priority lien against the assets of the business). A bank will consider the credit history, income and assets of the buyer, as well as the operating results and financial condition of the company.

Conventional bank financing or a home equity line of credit may be available. However, conventional bank financing for small business acquisitions is rare, and an SBA 7(a) loan is often the only bank financing available for a business acquisition. Note that SBA regulations generally require that a buyer be rejected by a conventional lender before they can qualify for an SBA 7(a) loan (i.e., the "lender of last resort"). SBA loans often provide lower rates than other commercial loans.

Many banks can facilitate an SBA loan or a loan under a similar state program. Certain banks are "preferred" SBA lenders and others are "approved" SBA lenders. Before your buyer spends too much time seeking financing, they should investigate which preferred banks in your community underwrite the most SBA 7(a) loans.

While loans under government programs may require more red tape, they often include business counseling or mentoring programs. Particularly in situations with business succession to current management or family members, these crucial business management skills may be missing. A buyer who succeeds operating your business is much more likely to pay the full purchase price.

Seller Financing

Seller financing is most common with the sale of smaller businesses and in cases where the owner sells the business to current members of management or their own family members. The seller of a Main Street business should be prepared to finance a portion of the sale (i.e., carry a note).

Seller financing comes with credit risk. You are lending to the buyer. Therefore, with the sale of a middle-market business, you need to think like a banker and secure your loan.

Even with a security interest over the business assets as collateral, you won't want to ultimately foreclose on your lien and recover the assets you just sold. You want to be paid the full purchase price in cash.

Find out why the buyer cannot borrow the full purchase price from a bank. This information will be enlightening. Insist that the buyer makes a substantial down payment on the purchase price — skin in the game which is lost upon a default.

Negotiate as many of the following terms as possible to protect your interests as a lender:

• Seek an irrevocable bank letter of credit payable upon default.

• Obtain a lien and security interest on the stock you sell and the assets of the company.

• Have the buyer personally guarantee the loan. If the buyer parent company sets up a new entity to purchase your business, get a guarantee from the parent company and major shareholders. The guarantors of the note should have adequate net worth to pay the note. If they don't have adequate net worth you effectively limit your recourse to the assets of the business. If you accept such a nonrecourse sale, you should receive an additional premium in the selling price.

• The loan should be documented in a promissory note with monthly payments of principal and interest. The note should bear interest at no less than the buyer's cost of capital. Otherwise, the buyer will have no incentive to prepay the note. If the buyer defaults, the note should accelerate.

• Try to avoid allowing the buyer the right to offset other claims against payments due on the note. Seek a negotiable note which would allow you to transfer the note.

• Require the buyer to accept positive and negative covenants, just like loan covenants.

• Require cross-defaults tied to the buyer's other loans and ancillary agreements, such as an employment agreement or lease.

Seller financing is often part of the purchase price because it is the only way to get the deal done. Particularly in the case of a sale to key employees, the buyers lack the cash and access to capital to deliver the full purchase price at closing. Require a significant portion of the purchase price to be paid by the buyer in cash at closing or you will continue to carry significant risks.

Buyer Retirement Funds

A buyer would incur huge tax penalties if they liquidated their retirement accounts and used the funds to buy your business. Recently, buyers have been able to use Rollovers as Business Startups ("ROBS") to fund an acquisition, wherein funds from eligible retirement accounts are rolled over and used to buy an existing business.

The steps are relatively simple. A new C corporation is formed. Then, a new 401(k) plan is created for this C corporation. The buyer's previous retirement accounts are rolled into the new 401(k) plan. These rolled-over retirement funds are used to purchase shares of stock of the C corporation. The funds from the sale of stock to the new 401(k) plan provide the cash used to buy the business. In the end, your business would be purchased by the new C corporation which is owned by the new 401(k) plan.

In addition to putting the buyer's retirement at a concentrated risk, the IRS has raised concerns about these plans, so a buyer should get legal and tax advice.

Mergers

A merger is an exchange of the stock of the acquiring company for stock of the target company at an exchange ratio that has been agreed upon. The target corporation disappears and is legally absorbed into the acquiring corporation. The merger may include a cash component paid to acquire the target. If the acquiring company will pay any cash in a merger this is usually paid from their corporate treasury or comfortably financed through their credit facilities.

The target shareholders will receive stock of the acquiring company which should have a known market value (for a publicly traded company). The current market price of the acquiring company's stock — relative to the acquiring company's management's perception of their own stock value — may drive the structure of a transaction toward a merger. If the acquiring company believes its stock currently has a high market price, then it is perceived by the buyer to be a good "currency" to use for acquisitions.

A merger is a choice to sell your business and a decision to "invest" in the stock of the acquiring company, since you will become a shareholder. (Would you sell your business to Tesla for $8 million in cash, and then invest all $8 million in Tesla stock?) Accordingly, the owners of the target company should complete their own due diligence before investing in the stock of the acquiring company. If the acquiring company is publicly traded, enough information may be available through the Securities and Exchange Commission and its EDGAR online database.

What goes up can come down, and many target company owners have become overnight multi-millionaires but lost their paper wealth when the market corrected. In the case of many asset bubbles (dotcom, energy, financial institutions, real estate, etc.) when the going is good, the deals are rampant. The art (and often luck) is to avoid holding overvalued assets when the music stops and taking substantial losses.

The dot-com bubble was a mix of rampant initial public offerings, subsequent trading at inflated prices and use of the dot-com's stock to acquire smaller businesses, generating overnight paper millionaires and overnight mega-losses.

With risks come rewards, and hot markets might be the best time for you to sell. May the force be with you.

A merger may follow a stock sale in a two-step transaction. The buyer may purchase the stock of the target company first, then merge the target (now a wholly owned subsidiary) into the acquiring/parent company. Once the acquiring company owns 100% of your stock, what the buyer does with the corporations is of little (or no) consequence to you.

Management Buyout

You might structure a succession plan to sell your ownership in your company to successors you have known for years – family members or key management. The new owners would pay you for your shares. The payoff for your shares is likely to come through a promissory note over several years, secured with your shares of the stock and the assets of the company.

Alternatively, you might structure a succession plan where you sell your ownership in your company back to the corporation itself. At the same time, the corporation could issue new shares to your successors. The corporation would pay you for the price of your shares.

A business shouldn't keep enough cash in the bank to buy out its owners in a single transaction. As described below, the company may borrow from a bank or other lender to pay a portion of your purchase price. However, the payoff for your shares is likely to come over a period of years through a promissory note payable to you from the company. The majority of your seller's note would be paid through future cash flows generated by the company. Again, your note should be secured with the assets of the company and a lien on your stock.

If your company is an S corporation, the repurchase of your shares by the company may generate long-term capital gains. If your company is a C corporation and it repurchases your shares in blocks over time, you may trigger ordinary income. To minimize ordinary income, you may need to structure the transaction to sell more of your shares in one transaction, so that you end up owning less than 50% of the outstanding shares and less than 80% of the number of shares you held before the repurchase.

Selling to your key employees who use internally generated cash flow to pay the purchase price is a risky exit strategy. You would continue to bear the risk of the success or failure of the business. This is a worthy option only if you have no alternative to sell to external buyers or if you are so loyal to your key employees that you are willing to bear this risk.

Institutional or Mezzanine Financing for a Buyout

If your middle-market business has sufficient cash flow or assets, your key employees may find institutional financing to fund a management buyout (MBO) or a leveraged buyout (LBO). The difference between an MBO and an LBO is the percentage of equity held by management at the end of the transaction. Institutional lenders will not typically invest in transactions below $5 million or $10 million.

In such an institutional transaction, the senior lenders will lend to your company based on its assets or cash flows so that the company can repurchase your stock with the proceeds of this loan. If your company has positive growth but insufficient assets or cash flows for institutional lenders, "mezzanine" lenders (usually unsecured and subordinated to senior lenders) may be willing to fund such an MBO or LBO.

Your company should retain enough cash following the purchase of your shares to remain solvent and pay debts as they become due. Otherwise, creditors may claim that your ownership has been transferred in a fraudulent transaction

Recapitalization

A leveraged recapitalization is similar to an institutional MBO or LBO, but you would retain control of your business after some of your stock is repurchased by the company using cash from the institutional loan. However, the lenders will require you to honor restrictive debt covenants to protect their loan.

Employee Stock Ownership Plan

If your business brings in revenue of $5 million or more, an Employee Stock Ownership Plan (or "ESOP") may be an attractive option as your exit plan. Technically a type of employee retirement program, an ESOP is expressly designed to enable a shareholder to liquidate their stock, using unique tax advantages that are associated with the ESOP's status as a "tax-qualified retirement plan".

How an ESOP works

To cash in stock via an ESOP, the business owner (with the help of a qualified attorney) would establish an employee stock ownership trust and appoint an individual or trust company as its trustee. The owner can then make an offer to the trustee to sell stock to the trust, where the shares would then be deposited to individual retirement accounts set up for each of the company's employees. Key considerations in selling stock to an ESOP include:

- **Setting the stock price.** The rules for ESOPs provide that the ESOP trustee must hire a professional, independent business appraiser to determine the fair market value of the stock that the owners wishes to sell. This determination of value then establishes the price that the trustee can offer for the stock.
- **How much stock to sell.** An attractive feature of an ESOP is that the trustee will purchase whatever portion of stock the owner may want to sell, whether that be one percent of the company, 100%, or anything in between. Thus, many business owners use an ESOP to "take some

chips off the table", initially liquidating 25-50% of their ownership, with the option to sell more shares later.

• **Financing the ESOP purchase.** The purchase money is not raised by the company's employees. Instead, the ESOP's purchase is financed either by a bank loan provided to the ESOP (using the company's credit) or by credit extended by the selling shareholder. Thus, the seller accepts a promissory note that calls for the ESOP to pay off the purchase price in installments. Either way, the ESOP will take on debt – either to a bank or to the seller. The ESOP pays off that debt using its share of the company's profits. For example, if the ESOP has purchased 40% of the company's outstanding shares, it is then entitled to 40% of the company's profits, which it uses to pay off its debt.

Special ESOP Tax Benefits

The ESOP's ability to pay off the debt described above is greatly enhanced by the unique tax provisions that are applicable to ESOPs. These include:

• Full deductibility of the future company profits that are paid the ESOP. To enable the ESOP to make payments to the bank or the selling shareholder, the company will contribute the proportionate share of company profits to the ESOP. Even though that cash will be used to pay off the debt owed by the ESOP, those company profit contributions are fully tax-deductible for the company.

Thus, the company ends up paying much lower federal and state income taxes – savings that offset much of the cash contribution to the ESOP.

• **Permanent deferral of the seller's capital gains.** A unique provision in the federal tax code (mirrored in almost all state tax codes) provides that the seller can defer – permanently – the capital gains taxes that would normally be due on the sale of the owner's stock. In many states, the combined federal and state capital gains taxes can exceed 25% of the seller's gain. These taxes can be avoided on a sale to the ESOP.

• **Deferral of the employees' income taxes.** Generally, if a company awards stock to the employees in exchange for their services, the fair market value of that stock will be immediately taxable to the employee (that is, the value must be reported as compensation on the employee's W-2). Employees are likely to be unhappy about having to pay a significant tax bill with no extra cash to pay this liability. In contrast, with an ESOP, the employees will receive stock that is deposited in tax-deferred retirement accounts. Thus, they pay no taxes on the value of their shares until they eventually retire and receive the cash value of their stock. This is another valuable income tax deferral that makes for a winning equity incentive program.

• Employee performance and productivity gains. Numerous research studies have considered the effectiveness of employee stock ownership as an incentive to spur employee productivity and company performance. Those studies confirm that companies do indeed experience productivity gains, improved margins and faster growth when the employees have a significant stake in the company's financial success.

• **Costs to establish an ESOP.** Establishing an ESOP will require the input of an expert consultant, a specialized attorney, a professional trustee and a valuation firm. Fees for all these services may run in the range of $100,000 to $200,000. This is certainly real money, but it may be less than the costs of selling a middle-market business by other means.[24]

Summary

"When there is a deal, there is a way" to finance the transaction. Most sales transactions require analysis of multiple financing alternatives. The better you are educated about financing alternatives and working with the right professionals, the more likely you are to work co-operatively with your buyer toward a solution. If you are unable to find an independent buyer who can finance the acquisition of your business, you can consider succession to insiders: current management, your family or an ESOP.

Zack, Southern Electrical Supplies

RCK is a profitable business with consistent earnings, a strong balance sheet and consistent balances of cash, short-term debt and roughly $12 million of long-term debt. Due to its other recent acquisitions, RCK did not have enough cash reserves to pay the full $15.5 million due at closing.

RCK had several options to finance the acquisition of SES. With low interest rates and seeking to guarantee that the SES acquisition would be accretive to RCK's consolidated earnings, RCK issued $10 million of mezzanine debt which was underwritten and held by a regional bank. The bank held notes which were unsecured and subordinated to RCK's existing long-term debt, but still at moderate interest rates.

The regional bank analyzed SES's financial statements, tax returns and pro forma financial statements, and these bankers spoke with Zack about SES's operations and its future.

Harry, Elegant Catering

Indulge was a profitable catering business. Two of the owners were a father-son combination, and the father, Dr. Brennan, is a plastic surgeon. The pro forma financial statements and financial projections of the combined companies showed the enhanced profitability of the combined operations. Consolidating their businesses would eliminate pricing pressure and provide cost savings in centralized food preparation and administrative functions.

Two banks indicated their willingness to finance up to 80% of the acquisition price through SBA 7(a) loans, with personal guaranties of the loan by the three owners. However, the financing costs, with all interest and financing fees were well in excess of Dr. Brennan's fixed investment returns. Dr. Brennan also did not like the idea of signing a personal guaranty, so his attorney drafted loan documents for Dr. Brennan to loan 90% of the purchase price to Indulge.

Chapter Eleven:

THE PURCHASE AGREEMENT

The agreement to sell your business will be documented and memorialized in a formal contract in one of three possible structures: an asset purchase agreement, a merger agreement or a stock purchase agreement. This agreement will be drafted and accompanied by several schedules disclosing necessary information about the company.

The process for drafting a purchase agreement will differ for the sale of a Main Street business vs. the sale of a middle-market business. The form used for a Main Street business is more of template, often provided by a business broker, with much less input from lawyers and far fewer representations and warranties about the business (as discussed later in this chapter).

The appropriate structure for the deal will usually be driven by a mix of issues ranging from taxes, continuing liabilities, existing contracts or permits, and other legal issues. The structure of the deal should be agreed upon at the letter of intent stage, but subsequent due diligence or renegotiation may necessitate a change in the structure. You should consult with your attorney and tax advisor in advance of selecting the structure of the transaction as they can provide the best guidance for the specific needs and goals of your business sale.

The structure of each type of purchase agreement is similar. You should rely heavily on your attorney to draft or review the agreement, but if your attorney's services are only focused on drafting the agreement it may not reflect enough knowledge of the company or the details underlying the transaction.

A bridge stands strong and stable because the two opposed sides lean on each other. Separate attorneys representing the buyer and seller should generate a solid and balanced agreement reflecting terms the buyer and seller have hammered out. This process can sometimes lead to excessive negotiation over small points, but the buyer and seller should be keenly aware that time is money – their money.

The buyer's attorney usually delivers the first draft of a purchase agreement. If the seller uses a broker, the parties may start with a standard broker's form. Either way, both parties need the services of an M&A attorney to negotiate the details of the agreement.

The parties to the agreement can help mitigate time, costs and delays by staying involved and being decisive about the rewards they are seeking and the risks they are willing to bear. Hashing out terms of the deal at the LOI stage will save money when drafting the purchase agreement.

The Fundamental Deal Terms

The opening paragraph of the agreement will identify the parties to the sale and the date of the agreement. Next, a few recitals reflect the general nature of the transaction.

The *first major section* of the agreement will describe the nature of the transaction, whether it be an acquisition of assets and assumption of certain obligations of the selling company, a purchase of the stock of the company from the current shareholders or a merger of the target company into the acquiring company. Main Street businesses are almost always sold through asset sales.

The *second section* will set forth how the buyer will pay and how the seller will deliver control. This can be as simple as setting forth the purchase price, how much will be paid at closing in cash and a promissory note, and if some of the purchase price will be subject to a "holdback" and delivered later — typically 12 months after the closing.

If the sale is structured as an asset purchase or a stock purchase, the purchase price received from the buyer can be structured in roughly the same manner, but it will differ as to whether it is paid to the company or directly to the owners. The purchase price in an asset sale or stock sale may be based upon assumptions, like the closing date balances of inventory and "net working capital" (current assets minus current liabilities). Since the precise balance of inventory and net working capital may not be known on the closing date, the parties may agree to a post-closing adjustment of the purchase price and a means for "settling up".

The seller's deliverables will differ for asset sales and stock sales. In an asset sale, the seller is a company which sells substantially all of the assets used in the business. At closing, the seller will deliver a bill of sale for the assets (and an assignment and assumption agreement to assign existing contracts). In a stock sale, the selling shareholders sell their stock to the buyer. At closing, the selling shareholders will deliver their share certificates. The seller's tax liability on the proceeds of asset and stock sales may differ dramatically, which is another reason you should consult your attorney and tax advisor before any anticipated business sale.

In the *second section of a merger* agreement, the acquiring company exchanges its shares of stock for the stock of the target company at an agreed-upon exchange rate. The target company disappears and becomes part of the acquiring company. Two corporations "become one" and all the assets and liabilities of the target company become assets and liabilities of the acquiring (i.e., surviving) company. All the contracts of the target transfer to the acquiring company by operation of law.

A merger of equals is when two companies join forces to become a bigger player in their industry. Since this book is about "selling your business," our desired merger would be a larger business gobbling up a smaller business, delivering shares of stock which have a known market value (for example, Facebook acquiring Instagram).

In the second section, the parties will also agree upon a closing date, though this date can be modified through a mutual agreement. From the onset of negotiations, be firm about a drop-dead closing date or the buyer can treat the deal as an "option" to buy your company rather than a firm agreement to complete the sale. Signing the purchase agreement could effectively give the buyer an option to close the sale, so look for ways to limit the buyer's right to walk.

From your perspective, it's best for signing and closing to take place on the same date. The buyer will want time between signing and closing to justify the expense of funds spent on professional fees and due diligence. The agreement should terminate if the transaction has not closed by a specified date.

If you agree to allow time between signing and closing, be aware of the buyer's right to terminate the agreement (or "outs"). For example, if the buyer can terminate the transaction based upon their due diligence, the buyer should lose this right after a certain period. The buyer should also give prompt notice of issues discovered during due diligence, with an opportunity for the seller to correct such issues.

Representations and Warranties

The third section of the agreement is where you brew some coffee and sit down with your lawyer. This is where you make representations and warranties (or "reps and warranties") about your business. Have you done everything perfectly in accordance with every law since the day you started your business? That is nearly impossible. Is everything perfect in your relationships with all your customers, vendors, employees, government agencies and other parties? That is hard to know.

The "reps and warranties" will typically cover the following topics:

- Organization of the corporation and qualification to do business
- Power and authority; due authorization
- Title to the company's assets
- The agreement does not conflict with other obligations
- The company will obtain all consents necessary to close
- The company's stockholders' equity
- Compliance with laws
- Licenses and permits
- Financial statements; no undisclosed liabilities
- Taxes
- Accounts receivable
- Fixed assets and vehicles
- Intellectual property
- Contracts
- Litigation; judgments
- Insurance
- Employees; labor
- Benefit plans and ERISA
- Employee immigration matters
- Broker's fees and expenses
- Absence of material changes
- Bank accounts
- Affiliate transactions
- Real property
- Environmental
- Data Privacy

In addition, the seller will confirm they aren't leaving out representations necessary to "tell the whole story" considering the specific representations. This representation is breached by any incorrect representations or failure to disclose information necessary to make complete and correct representations, without showing you intentionally or recklessly misrepresented any facts.

The risk of litigation arising from inaccurate representations and warranties is why they require a careful review with and translation by your attorney.

Schedules, Exceptions and Knowledge Qualifiers

Schedules will be attached to the agreement. Every agreement has mandatory schedules listing bank accounts, major contracts, intellectual property, licenses and permits, employees, and other important items. You should be aware of numerous exceptions you will be obligated to carve out from various representations, and that is exactly what the agreement will reflect.

Such "exceptions" are also listed on these schedules. If a company is party to a lawsuit, the representation, "we have no lawsuits" will be revised to state "except as set forth on schedule 3.12, we have no lawsuits," and schedule 3.12 will reflect all the litigation.

This is like confession. Do not fail to disclose any known "exceptions". However, you should review the reps carefully with your lawyer, so you do not disclose any more nor any less than necessary.

Certain exceptions will apply to more than one representation. For example, pending litigation is also a contingent liability. You would need to reference this exception to both representations. As additional protection, your schedules should make clear that information set forth in the schedules modifies all representations, warranties and covenants in the agreement and none of these facts may be used as any claim against the seller. This may seem obvious, but without adding such language the legal presumption is not in the seller's favor.

Several reps will draw a natural response, "I have no idea." If you have a trademark, do you "know" that no one on earth is infringing on your trademark? Probably not. This is when you add the phrase "to the best of seller's knowledge" before a representation.

The buyer might not be willing to accept a "knowledge qualifier" for certain reps. In certain instances, a seller may need to represent facts without a knowledge qualifier simply because the buyer won't bear the risk of the unknown. Try to limit the scope of the individuals whose knowledge can be imputed to breaches of reps and warranties (ranging from only the owner to every officer of the selling company).

The reps and warranties reflect a major allocation of risk, like an insurance policy written by the seller with a specific list of exceptions. Just like an insurance company, it needs to be drafted carefully and skillfully to manage risks and limit liabilities.

If the parties ultimately cannot agree upon how to allocate risks under the reps and warranties, the parties may agree to purchase reps and warranties insurance so that the buyer is indemnified for any future losses arising under such contested reps and warranties. The parties would agree how to split the cost of such reps and warranties insurance.

If the buyer discovers breaches of reps and warranties before the closing, negotiate so that the buyer should not be able to close and sue based upon such known breaches.

In section four, the buyer will make representations and warranties, but these are far more limited than those made by the seller. After all, you are mainly concerned that their "money is green". The buyer typically represents the following:

- Organization of the corporation
- Power and authority; due authorization of the deal
- The agreement does not conflict with other obligations
- Broker's fees and expenses

If the seller breaches any representations and warranties, the buyer may have several options:

- Refuse to close
- Close and sue for damages
- If the sale has already closed when the breach is discovered, and the representation was material, rescind the transaction (unwind the deal).

None of these are attractive options, which is why you should list any known exceptions. You will need to remain apprised of the subject matter covered in the reps and warranties so that you can update them through the closing date.

Covenants and Conditions

Next, the agreement will reflect "covenants" stating what the parties will do and will refrain from doing between the date of execution and the date of closing. The parties may agree on covenants including the following:

- Completing due diligence.
- Both shall bear their own expenses doing the deal (advisors' fees).
- Payment of taxes.
- Conduct of business pending the closing (maintain the status quo).
- Certain pre-closing actions (specific changes to the status quo).
- Confidentiality and public announcements (keeping quiet about the sale until a joint announcement).
- Closing agreements (draft other agreements related to the sale, non-compete, employment, etc.)

The termination section will set forth conditions under which either party may walk from the deal. Termination is typically permitted under the following situations:

- If one party breaches and fails to "cure" their breach, the other may terminate.
- If the due diligence reflects major problems about the business, the buyer may terminate.

• If the deal fails to close by a certain date, either party may terminate.

As a corollary to termination, the closing of the deal will be conditioned upon the occurrence certain events:

• Representations and warranties are true.
• Due diligence has been completed.
• The parties will have performed and complied with all terms, conditions and obligations required by the agreement.
• The seller will have obtained any third-party consent required to close the sale (landlords and other contracts).
• There will be no legal action or proceedings to prohibit the sale.
• The company will not experience a "Material Adverse Effect" (a significant and adverse effect upon the company's assets or business operations) between signing and closing.

If delivery of an attorney's "legal opinion" is included among the conditions to close, be sure to agree upon the form of the opinion prior to signing. Otherwise, the final negotiation of the legal opinion can hold up closing.

Note that the buyer can typically refuse to close if the representations and warranties are not true on the closing date. If you are in a strong negotiating position, you may insist upon a "hell or high water" clause which will obligate the buyer to close the sale, whether the reps are correct on the closing date or not.

If the buyer retains the right to refuse to close, require written notice of their discovery of any inaccurate reps and an opportunity to cure. Furthermore, require the buyer's election to either waive and close the sale or terminate the agreement.

Indemnification

Indemnification sounds more dangerous and confusing that it really is. Claims or losses can and will arise after the closing of the sale. If a loss arises because of a breach of any term of the agreement, the party in breach must reimburse (i.e., indemnify) the other party for its loss. The seller will be liable for any breaches of representations and warranties, or any claims or obligations which were not assumed by the buyer. The buyer will be liable for any breaches of its representations and warranties or any claims or obligations which arise from business operations post-closing.

If a third-party lawsuit is brought against the business, expect the plaintiff to sue both the buyer and seller. If the events giving rise to the lawsuit arose before the closing, the seller should bear the burden of this claim (and indemnify the buyer for any costs). If the events giving rise to the lawsuit arose after the closing, the buyer should bear the burden of this claim (and indemnify the seller for any costs).

Lawsuits cost money, so the buyer and seller should try to present a unified front to defend the claims and use the same lawyer. If you are responsible for indemnification of a claim, you should be able to hire the attorney who will primarily defend the case so that you can control the costs of defense. The buyer may also be represented by counsel to defend the case. After the claim is resolved, the parties can sort out who was responsible and settle-up.

Generally, any party who signs an agreement can be held liable. Try to avoid having your spouse sign the agreement. In a merger, since the merging entity disappears, its shareholders are the ones who can be held liable. A minority shareholder should try to limit their liability proportionately to their percentage ownership of the company's stock.

Rights to seek indemnification (and all liability under the agreement) should expire quickly for losses which would be apparent soon after the closing. Certain claims, like those for taxes, may not be known until years after closing and can be subject to a longer expiration period or default to the underlying statute of limitations. Total liability should be capped at some percentage of the purchase price. The seller's liability should never exceed the purchase price.

As a seller you will want to maintain insurance covering the business after closing which protects you against claims for which you may be liable. Be sure that the buyer obtains sufficient post-closing insurance and that you are named as an additional insured party.

Try to eliminate the buyer's right to rescind the sale based upon a material loss from any breach by the seller. If the buyer suffers a post-closing loss any resulting indemnification should be net of the tax benefit of the loss and net of any insurance proceeds received by the buyer.

General Sections and Drafting

The "general provisions" in the purchase agreement are the same types of bells and whistles included in all major contracts, such as the manner for providing notices to the other party, the controlling law and possibly an arbitration clause.

The drafting and negotiation of the purchase agreement is often a seller's least favorite aspect of selling a business. Get the right help from your attorney, but don't put your head in the sand. It's your money that will be subject to claims if the agreement and the schedules are not accurate. The risks are foreseeable and manageable if you get the right legal advice from the outset of negotiations.

Zack, Southern Electrical Supplies

Ten days after the letter of intent was signed, RCK's attorneys delivered a draft of an asset purchase agreement. The asset purchase agreement was reviewed by Zack, SES's M&A attorney and M&A advisor. Zack's M&A advisor provided high-level comments on the major terms, delivering them to the attorney.

Zack and the attorney discussed the most significant issues that were identified, including several representations and warranties and other sections which will require disclosure schedules, such as lists of major contracts and employees, and all exceptions to representations and warranties.

Zack instructed Ella to start preparing these schedules. Ella and an associate from their attorney's firm reviewed SES's contracts to identify all existing contracts which require the other party's consent before SES could assign the contracts to RCK. Other than SES's lease, only two agreements required consent to assignment. Since SES's attorney had always reviewed and edited all of SES's major contracts, most all its contracts either allowed assignment or only required that SES notify the other party of the assignment.

SES's attorney added "knowledge qualifiers" to all the representations where Zack could not identify any specific exceptions, but he was unsure of their truth. SES's attorney integrated all the comments and sent a redlined version of the agreement back to RCK's attorney.

After two more revisions to the agreement, the attorneys and parties had eliminated all the remaining differences between them. SES's attorney delivered drafts of the disclosure schedules with the final version of the agreement that he revised.

RCK's attorney delivered drafts of all "ancillary agreements" related to the asset purchase, such as the bill of sale, assignment and assumption agreement, consulting agreement and a non-compete agreement. SES's attorney provided minimal comments on these drafts, most of which were accepted by RCK's attorney. The ancillary agreements and revised disclosure schedules were added as exhibits to the execution version of the asset purchase agreement which was circulated to the parties for execution.

Both corporations obtained unanimous written consent from their boards of directors to execute these agreements.

Finally, Zack and RCK's CEO executed the asset purchase agreement three weeks after it was first drafted by RCK's attorney. The agreement reflected balanced negotiation and appropriate allocations of risk between the parties. Zack was obligated to sign the agreement on behalf of all the SES corporations and as an individual. However, Zack's wife, Kelly, was not required to sign the agreement.

Harry, Elegant Catering

Since Harry was represented by a business broker, his broker prepared a standard purchase agreement on a form developed by his brokerage firm, inserting the names of the parties, the purchase price and a target closing date of April 1, 2020. The broker's form was drafted much like a real estate purchase agreement with emphasis on the conditions to closing and forfeiture of a large deposit if the buyer failed to close.

The buyers were represented by an attorney who objected to the use of this form. The buyers' attorney asserted that he should provide a draft of the purchase agreement, which is the standard process in a transaction where attorneys represent the parties. Harry insisted that he would not hire an attorney and would not consider a purchase agreement drafted by the buyers.

The buyers' attorney reviewed the broker's form of asset purchase agreement and provided an extensive markup of comments along with riders typed up for addition or substitution. Harry's broker was unwilling to respond to the buyers' attorney's comments, saying he was unqualified to address legal issues.

Harry acted as his own attorney and reviewed the buyers' revisions to the purchase agreement. Harry did not understand the significance of the changes proposed by the buyers' attorney and, being eager to close the sale, he accepted all the changes.

Chapter Twelve:

DUE DILIGENCE

After signing a purchase agreement to buy a house, you have it inspected by an expert. Based on what you discover, you can walk away from the deal, demand repairs or ask for a reduction of the price for repairs which aren't completed. Due diligence is a similar process for business sales.

Due diligence is the "heavy lifting" necessary to complete the sale. It is for the buyer's benefit, but the seller will closely monitor the due diligence to control disclosure of sensitive information and prevent any premature announcement of the sale. Due diligence is a thorough process, so you should expect all the strengths and weaknesses of your business to be laid bare.

Much like dating prior to marriage, it is not possible to expect to hide your defects all the way through to your wedding day. The key is to spark the buyer's desire to buy your business before they become aware of its defects. At the right time, reveal any defects directly to the buyer so they don't feel as though you have misled them.

Satisfy the Buyer's Need for Information

The buyer of your business can be viewed as a major customer. You seek something from the buyer: a large sum of money. The buyer wants something from you: information about your business.

The purpose of the buyer's due diligence is to corroborate the information you have already provided, and dig for more, enough so that the buyer feels relatively confident that they know all the crucial facts about your business and appreciate the risks in acquiring your business. In almost every transaction which isn't a fire sale liquidation, the buyer's offer is contingent upon the successful completion of their due diligence review.

Just like you assemble an M&A Team to facilitate the sale, the buyer's team will divide their due diligence work and review all the legal, accounting, sales, human resources, and operating data you provide.

Prepare for and Manage the Due Diligence Process

Some portion or all of the buyer's due diligence may be completed before the purchase agreement is signed. This will reduce the volume of due diligence review between signing and closing and the likelihood that the buyer will walk away from a signed purchase agreement. Early due diligence generally includes financial accounting and information that is less sensitive to share.

The seller needs to quickly provide documents requested by the buyer. The seller is required to invest significant time including the owner, management, employees, attorneys and other professionals. For larger companies, the seller's cost of the due diligence can run into six figures. This six-figure expenditure is usually unbudgeted and can put a significant financial strain on the company's operational cash.

Most due diligence is done after a potential buyer has made an offer, and much of the due diligence comes after the execution of the LOI and before the purchase agreement is signed. The due diligence process can take from 30 to 90 days.

Due diligence will be less of a burden if you start preparations early. With advance preparation, the disclosure process can be performed over a reasonable period which should not put undue stress on the seller.

A good goal for the due diligence process is to have your company prepare, in advance, 80% to 85% of the materials your prospective buyer will request. Advance preparation will make the process much easier for both you and the buyer. This goal will also separate and distinguish your business from the competition, making it more attractive to the prospective buyer. An example of a due diligence request list is included as Appendix C to aid your advance preparation.

Due Diligence Nightmares

To properly plan for due diligence, you should know how quickly the process can deteriorate:

The following scene has been played out countless times: an investor approaches the business owner with an offer that seems attractive. They go out for a wonderful lunch or dinner—the great seduction scene. The personal chemistry is excellent, consensus emerges quickly, and the parties map out a deal on the back of a napkin. They shake hands on the general framework of a deal, perhaps even agree on the value of the business, and depart thinking that the deal is done, subject only to some minor details.

Then the investor starts with his or her Due Diligence. A trickle of questions turns into an endless stream. One set of answers leads to another set of questions. The stream turns into a torrent. The barrage of questions puts serious pressure on company management.

The [prospective buyer] becomes frustrated with the slow pace at which the incomplete information is provided, and with the ambiguity or inaccuracy, or perhaps even contradictory nature, of the information received. The owner becomes frustrated with the resources consumed, and often misconstrues the questions as a lack of trust or failing commitment on the part of the investor.

If the initial waves of questions are answered satisfactorily, the investor goes on to appoint legal advisors and auditors, who then unleash further extensive waves of newer and even more complicated and more detailed questions.

Whole teams of advisors descend upon the company, taking information demands to new heights. Company management is under huge stress after all, managers have a business to run, yet satisfying the investor turns into more than a full-time job. Tensions mount. More often than not, negotiations break off sometimes in an emotional or dramatic showdown or the parties may just give up from exhaustion or frustration.[25]

With proper planning, you can avoid this nightmare destruction of your sale. Assemble the necessary records, identify those which contain the most sensitive information and control the release of documentation. Do not release information too early, but do not stonewall your buyer.

Due Diligence Request Lists

The buyer or their attorney will deliver a lengthy due diligence request list. (See Appendix C.) These lists typically cover the following topics, and include specific requests within each category:

o General information about the company's structure
o Management and employees
o Products and services
o Competition
o Customer information
o Key vendors and service providers

o Technology, software and hardware

o Marketing, branding and public relations

o Related parties and minority owners

o Insurance

o Financial information

o Inventory

o Intellectual property and intangible assets

o Contracts and leases

o Litigation and claims

o Taxes

o Environmental

The list of due diligence requests will be generated using a template, a comprehensive list reflecting everything under the sun about a generic business, but then it is narrowed to reflect the issues applicable to your business. A software development firm probably has little to no environmental risk while an agricultural wholesale business may not have intellectual property issues. Nevertheless, the buyer's advisors need to show they have covered everything:

> Most owners are shocked by the depth and breadth of the due diligence process. This process of "full and fair" disclosure enables a buyer to verify all provided data and reviews all information about the company. All includes anything that would interest the buyer at any level.

> Most business owners are highly independent people who find this disclosure process extremely uncomfortable.[26]

The simple solution to address inapplicable due diligence requests for information is to respond in writing and explain why such requests do not generate any documents for the seller to produce. Usually the inapplicable request will be laid to rest. Fighting over non-issues is counterproductive and only raises more questions.

Disclosing Confidential Information

You will need an orderly process for disclosing information to the buyer and keeping confidential your sensitive information. You must adequately protect your company's confidential information. After all, this is your information, and nobody has a right to see it until you give the approval.

The "data room" will contain many of your company's most important documents. It may contain trade secrets, intellectual property, and other confidential information that makes your company unique.

Formality is important in this step and coordination with your attorney and other members of your M&A Team is paramount. Rely upon your M&A attorney or M&A advisor to control the disclosure of key documents and proprietary information.

However, the sale is unlikely to close if the buyer isn't given access to all crucial information. Let's assume the role is reversed and you are going to purchase a company. Both you and the seller would sign the appropriate nondisclosure agreements. Then you would have the expectation that you and your M&A Team would have access to the seller's documents. You would assume that the information should be easily accessible.

You should also have privacy when you and your M&A Team discuss the documents provided by the seller.

Protect your sensitive information, but understand the buyer's need to review virtually everything, and provide the most sensitive information as the deal becomes more certain.

Virtual Data Room

With today's technology, the delivery of documents can be done in the "cloud".

The due diligence process is a massive document management and access security project. You and your M&A Team should consider using a Virtual Data Room (VDR) instead of a physical room with reams of documents. A VDR offers numerous benefits, as long as necessary legal nondisclosure and IT security measures are in place.

> As the name suggests, a virtual data room, or as it is more frequently called, a "VDR," is an online database in which companies can store and share confidential information, usually used during a financial transaction. It may also be described as a type of electronic repository or document filing system. With the ubiquitous reliance on computers and specialized software to keep a business running smoothly, coupled with the fact that more and more companies are making the transition to a completely paperless office, many of the previously document-heavy

operational practices have been shifted to the virtual realm.

VDRs are used by companies to securely store and share critical and sensitive corporate data and are most commonly used during deals. The information stored in a data room is generally private documentation that is typically considered to be of high value to the company or owner of the data room. Of course, in addition to traditional record keeping that is required for many financial, legal, and tax matters, a lot of companies have other important documents and information that they need to retain and would like to store safely to ensure that it remains confidential. For example, items relating to intellectual property, such as trade secrets and copyrighted works must be convenient to access but also stored in a highly secure location. Because of the growing importance of data and the ensuing increased demand to ensure that such data is adequately safeguarded, the virtual data room was born, and over the years, it has evolved into the kind of solution that it is today.

For financial transactions, virtual data room software has become the norm, replacing the once-ubiquitous physical data rooms. Physical data rooms had their limitations and were time consuming and inconvenient for the parties involved. With the advancement of online security (which is of paramount importance to virtual data rooms), the physical data room became an outdated concept, being replaced with a virtual deal room, where companies could share due diligence information securely and from anywhere in the world.[27]

Some of the key issues for analysis of the viability of a VDR include the following:

- Access and security.
- Whether the VDR is cloud-based or locally hosted.
- Scanning and uploading documents into the VDR.
- Validating that each document is properly stored on the VDR.
- Providing the buyer access to the data.
- Backup of all documents on the VDR.

In addition to a VDR, you may wish to retain your most sensitive information in hard copies and limit review access to a physical room, possibly one located at your attorney's office.

Zack, Southern Electrical Supplies

After signing a non-disclosure agreement, RCK received SES's financial statements. After the letter of intent was signed, SES delivered its tax returns, corporate minutes, real estate lease and equipment leases.

Zack and his M&A attorney identified SES's most sensitive or proprietary information, including its customer lists, employment records and attorney-client records. In addition, SES identified business records for which it agreed to maintain confidentiality for other businesses and individuals.

Attorneys for RCK delivered a comprehensive due diligence request list when delivering the initial draft of the purchase agreement. SES delivered nearly all the requested documents or written responses indicating why such requests were inapplicable, and it withheld its most sensitive business records.

SES's business records were delivered by its M&A attorney through a cloud based VDR. RCK had a team of attorneys, finance and operations personnel, who divided and reviewed the mass of SES's records. SES responded promptly to all RCK's follow-up questions and requests.

After the purchase agreement was signed and RCK secured its mezzanine financing, SES allowed RCK's attorneys and its top management to visit the office of SES's M&A attorney, so they could review hard copies of the most sensitive information. RCK's CFO joined their corporate attorneys to review these records, but they raised no concerns.

After Zack provided his permission, RCK's top management was given permission to interview the other management of SES. He also gave RCK permission to speak with two of SES's largest customers.

Harry, Elegant Catering

In May 2019, Harry saw his first potential buyer, Mac, terminate the sale after learning of Elegant Catering's poor accounting practices, delinquent tax returns and the ongoing employee misclassification audit by the IRS and the California EDD.

After the February 2020 letter of intent was signed with the owners of Indulge, the buyers' attorney delivered a due diligence request list to Harry's broker. Following the buyers' execution of a non-disclosure agreement, Harry's broker delivered all of Elegant Catering's tax returns and financial statements since its inception. Concerned that the recent tax returns showed lower net income than they were led to believe, the buyers threatened to terminate the sale.

Harry and his broker met again with the buyers and their attorney. Harry looked desperate to sell Elegant Catering. The buyers offered to reduce the price to $800,000 fixed and a $200,000 earn-out. Harry's broker said this was bad faith and beneath the defensible valuation of $1 million. Harry insisted the price remain $1 million fixed, but he was willing to drop the earn-out. The buyers left with no agreement on the price.

That evening, Harry's broker called the buyers' attorney and salvaged a deal with a fixed price of $800,000 and a $300,000 earn-out.

After the purchase agreement was signed, Harry's broker delivered copies of Elegant Catering's lease, two other contracts, the LLC's operating agreement and the settlement agreement to buy out Skip. Finally, after deliberating with Harry, his broker delivered all records related to the IRS and EDD employee misclassification audit. The IRS and EDD had completed their work in November 2019, imposing total employment taxes, penalties and interest of $174,000, agreeing to a three-year payment plan bearing interest at 7.75%. Seeing these employment issues gave the buyers renewed pause.

After the buyers again threatened to terminate the sale, Harry agreed to reduce the fixed portion of the purchase price to $700,000 and sign an indemnification agreement drafted by the buyers' attorney. The agreement covered not only employment related liabilities but any liabilities from Elegant Catering's operations (and even certain post-closing liabilities). Harry was perplexed by the 12-page indemnification agreement, but being desperate to sell, he signed it.

The buyers were frustrated that most of their due diligence requests were left unsatisfied. Harry's business records were disorganized or nonexistent, and his broker's response to most requests was simply "n/a." After making renewed requests and threatening to terminate the sale, the buyers decided to rely upon the one-sided indemnification agreement and reductions to the purchase price.

Chapter Thirteen:

REACH THE CLOSING

In theory, the closing should be the easiest part of the transaction: an exchange of signed documents and certificates, delivery of the purchase price in exchange for the bill of sale or stock certificates. The focus of this chapter is the final scramble to reach closing and the interminable post-closing actions necessary to settle-up with the buyer and complete the transfer of your business.

As the closing date becomes imminent, the final preparation for closing can become stressful. Your M&A Team will need to roll up their sleeves and dive into the details while doing some final clean-up.

During due diligence, the buyer or their counsel will discover a list of issues. Some of these hiccups will require fixing, and some will be used by the buyer to lower the purchase price or hold back more of the cash.

Your accounting staff will need to work overtime as the closing day nears. Your team will probably need to adjust the final account balances on your balance sheet, particularly current assets and liabilities (payables and receivables). You will need an accurate net working capital balance before closing to avoid a material post-closing adjustment to the purchase price or a dispute with your buyer.

Consent to Assignment of Leases and Other Contracts

If you are selling through the most common form of transaction—an asset sale—you may need to obtain consent to assignment from several contractual counterparties. You should unearth the list of contracts which require consent to assignment through the due diligence process.

Landlords generally require their consent to assign the lease even with a stock sale or merger (since their consent is usually required for any transaction which constitutes a "change in control" of the company).

In addition to consent from your landlord, countless other contracts—particularly those executed with sophisticated businesses—require consent to assignment. Failing to obtain required consent would be a breach of your purchase agreement (and a breach of such contracts) which would expose you to liabilities.

Many of your contractual counterparties will be slow to deliver their consent to assignment or hold-outs may demand payment to grant their consent. Be prepared for the closing by rounding up all necessary consents early in the process. Your business will request and obtain from your contractual counterparties consent to assign such contracts to the buyer of your business.

The parties may also find that key contracts or agreements with employees were never signed. Hopefully this can be resolved quickly.

Other existing contracts may be incompatible with the buyer's business for a variety of reasons, and it may be necessary to amend the contract. If your contract counterparty is a good business partner, an amendment may come easily. Other amendments may require renegotiation.

Your landlord's consent will be necessary to assign your lease (or a new lease may be required). If the buyer is less credit-worthy than your business, expect some negotiations with your landlord. A landlord can throw a wrench in the sale of a business by withholding their consent to assignment.

Your landlord should be approached about the need for their consent at "the right time". A landlord shouldn't be approached when a deal is still speculative, at the LOI and early negotiation stages. After the agreement is signed and the bulk of due diligence has been successfully completed, the deal has reached a critical mass.

Just like a daughter who waits until things have gotten serious to bring her boyfriend home to meet the parents, her parents are less likely to disapprove of him.

However, don't delay closing by approaching the landlord too late and causing unnecessary anxiety for everyone involved. Waiting too late creates the appearance that you aren't allowing your landlord enough time to consider the buyer's credit or trying to "pull a fast one".

Your experienced advisors should help you determine the right time to approach your landlord. If you are being acquired by a large business, your landlord may be delighted to have a financially sound new tenant.

Your landlord will often have their own attorney assist with a lease assignment and recover this cost from you.

Statutory Closing Conditions

If your sale would cause a plant closing or mass layoffs, statutory requirements, including the U.S. Worker Adjustment and Retraining Notification Act (the "WARN Act"), would require 60 days of notice to employees and local government authorities. If you are party to a merger which is subject to the Hart-Scott Rodino Act, you must complete a 30-day waiting period and premerger notifications with the Federal Trade Commission and the Antitrust Division of the Justice Department.

Web and Cloud Assets and Accounts

The website, URL, the hosting and email accounts are all business assets which the buyer will want to acquire. Many business owners use their work email as their primary email account and don't realize this email will be transferred to the buyer at closing. Take appropriate corrective measures to back up emails onto your home computer and delete personal emails stored on your work account.

Similarly, take corrective measures to secure control over all the "virtual assets" the buyer will need so that you can deliver all the necessary details: contact information, usernames and password of all websites, email hosting cloud server accounts.

Personal Guaranties

Prior to closing, you should be released from personal guaranties with banks, landlords, licenses and similar obligations. Indemnification by the buyer is not nearly as good as being released from such obligations. If the buyer's credit is insufficient to allow for your release from obligations to third parties, you should reconsider the value of the buyer's obligation to indemnify you.

Announcing the Sale

Prior to the closing, you want to keep your business intact and operating. Employees should not be made aware of the sale until as late as possible. If employees, customers and competitors learn that your business is for sale, you could suffer significant harm.

Employees who discover their place of employment is being sold become worried and start exploring alternatives. Those employees who discover that a potential sale fell through may lose confidence in the stability of their employment. Customers may start doing business with your competitors.

The buyer also doesn't want to destroy your business before the closing, but the buyer will want to speak with key employees to know who will stay and who will go. Similarly, the buyer may want to speak with key customers (and possibly vendors) to confirm these relationships won't be adversely affected by the sale.

Some business owners wait until the closing date to tell their employees. It's an art to properly time all these announcements to various parties. Once the initial announcement is made outside your inner circle, expect the news to spread like wildfire.

In every asset sale, employees are formally terminated by the selling corporation and rehired by the buyer. Be prepared to cut their final paychecks with all accrued benefits in accordance with all employment laws.

Post-Closing Payments

Net Working Capital Adjustments

The purchase price may be based upon an assumed balance of net working capital (current assets minus current liabilities). The actual balance of net working capital will not be known and agreed upon until the books are closed and reconciled.

The parties typically agree upon a method to settle-up on the difference between the actual net working capital and the assumed net working capital balance. This usually happens a month or two after closing, with another month allowed to resolve disagreements over the balance of net working capital.

Inventory

If your business carries inventory for resale, the purchase agreement may reflect the amount of inventory, at cost, that must be on hand on the closing date. This should be the inventory level maintained by the business in the normal course of doing business. Often the parties jointly take inventory on the closing date. If the inventory is below the balance specified in the purchase agreement, the proceeds from the sale are reduced by the shortage. Conversely, if the inventory at closing exceeds the specified level, the proceeds from the sale are adjusted upward by the amount of the surplus.

Holdback payments

The buyer will want to retain a portion of the purchase price to provide security against undisclosed liabilities and claims that might come out of the woodwork. The buyer's rights to recover for such losses are set forth in the indemnification section, but no buyer wants to spend years in court suing to recover a portion of the purchase price from you. The buyer assumes you will be lying on the beach enjoying fruity cocktails for the rest of your life.

The buyer will often hold a portion of the purchase price for payment approximately one year after the closing date in order to have security, deduct and offset their losses against such future payment. You will have the right to dispute any offsets taken against future payments. The parties will agree upon a method for resolving disagreements over these losses. The holdback sum might be deposited with a third-party escrow or simply a promise to pay from the buyer.

Holdback payments are a reasonable way for a buyer to protect themselves against the unknown. The holdback payments are typically delivered to the seller a year or more after the closing date.

Earn-outs

Earn-outs are not for protection. When an earn-out is included in the purchase price, it is a used to reduce the fixed purchase price and share some of the future profits with the seller. Earn-outs can be used to bridge the gap between the parties' divergent valuations of the business. Earn-outs may give the seller more incentive to support the business going forward, but you must accept that control over profitability is usually lost at closing.

Earn-outs are portions of the purchase price which are linked to the company's operating results for a given period after closing, often several future periods of time. An earn-out may be tied to future revenue or earnings. Revenue balances are the least likely to generate a dispute over the amount of the earn-out. As the parties move farther down the company's income statement for the income-measure used to calculate the earn-out (net income or EBITDA rather than revenue or gross profits) they are more likely to have a dispute over the earn-out.

The buyer will have control over expenses and the accounting for expenses. This allows for manipulation of the earn-out calculation. The buyer has an incentive to invest in research & development and marketing during the earn-out period, depressing short-term earnings for long-term benefit, and reducing the earn-out payment.

To avoid such manipulation, you can agree with the seller to limit such expenditures or exclude them from the calculation of the earn-out. You might try to protect payment of the earn-out by receiving regular periodic payments, prohibit payment of distributions until the earn-out is paid or escrowing a balance for payment of the earn-out.

If your business is acquired by a larger company or a strategic buyer, beware of allocation of the buyer's overhead as well as transactions between the acquired business and the buyer's affiliates. The buyer should maintain the same accounting methods which you used, such as inventory accounting.

The earn-out may be beyond your control and although it might be a potentially large sum, it is money you may not receive. The earn-out is gravy, the icing on the cake.

Additional Contracts

In addition to the purchase agreement (which is the key agreement in the transaction) the parties will execute other contracts. The parties to the sale will also execute a variety of other instruments or certificates to give effect to the closing.

Employment Agreement or Consulting Agreement

The buyer might want you to remain employed with the business for a certain period after the closing. You might want job security if you are willing to postpone your endless rounds of golf or your trip sailing around the world. Thus, an employment contract is common if the seller will remain employed post-closing.

This agreement will set forth the duties you will have on the job and expectations of both parties about your working conditions. It should specify a term of employment, such as one to three years. You cannot be legally forced to work against your will, and the buyer will not want an obligation to keep you employed past the "Honeymoon" period. If your employment is terminated before the end of the agreed-upon period, you will typically receive a severance package.

Often it is difficult for business owners to move down the chain in command and under new leadership. Similarly, soon after they are comfortable managing their new business, the new owners find they have "too many cooks in the kitchen".

Get legal advice from an employment attorney to understand the true meaning of your employment agreement. A five-year contract is not a guaranteed salary for five years. Try to limit the buyer's ability to move your place of employment to a new location, narrow the definition of termination "for cause", require continuation of the benefits you need, and condition your non-compete provision on payment of your salary and benefits.

If the parties do not wish to maintain an employment relationship post-closing, a consulting agreement may be a better alternative.

It is rare for a business owner to hand over control and flee from the scene with no continuing obligation to provide services. At a minimum, you should expect to be obligated to make yourself available for consulting and support for 30 days or more. If your purchase price includes an earn-out, it is in your best interests to ensure a smooth and profitable transition.

Non-compete Agreement

The buyer would not succeed in operating your business if you open a competing business right next door after the closing. The buyer needs assurance that you won't take your expertise and relationships to build a competitor and thereby destroy the value of the business you sold.

The law in most states will not allow enforcement of non-compete provisions within employment agreements because people need to be able to work to contribute to society. Similarly, non-compete agreements executed as part of business sales are subject to legal limits in many states, such as reasonable periods of time and geographic areas.

A court may look to the nature of the transaction and the total purchase price to determine if a non-compete agreement is fully enforceable. A buyer may want to include language so that the non-compete agreement will be enforced to the maximum extent allowed rather than completely voided if it exceeds the legal limits.

If you will need to return to work in the same industry post-closing, negotiate in writing for any exceptions or limits to the non-compete. Do not reply upon the buyer's generosity after the deal is closed. If the buyer fails to deliver any payments owed post-closing, the non-compete agreement should terminate.

The parties may negotiate over whether post-closing compensation is a portion of the purchase price (for the seller's non-compete agreement), or a payment of salary and benefits post-closing.

The Escrow and Bulk Sales Process

To close a sale, a third party may perform the escrow function. This may be an attorney who holds executed documents in trust until all the closing conditions have been satisfied and all the necessary documentation has been received. Alternatively, this function may be served by an escrow agent, the type which also closes real estate transactions.

Not all real estate escrow agencies provide services for asset sales. Most escrow agents are limited to real estate transactions. If an escrow agent is necessary, the parties usually open escrow immediately after signing the purchase agreement.

An escrow agent is often unnecessary unless your business is subject to "bulk sales laws". Bulk sales laws are intended to protect creditors. Bulk sales laws apply to asset sales within a certain dollar range if your business makes most of its revenue selling products from inventory (or if you own a restaurant). The bulk sales process takes approximately 30 days. You will deliver a list of creditors to the escrow agent. All known creditors receive notice of the sale and another notice is published in the newspaper.

Creditors will return a demand for payment to be paid through the escrow. If the bulk sales laws apply to your asset sale, failure to comply with these laws will leave the buyer liable to all the seller's creditors. Thus, it's usually the buyer who pushes for an escrow and bulk sale notice to be included in the deal.

Escrow Agreements and Promissory Notes

If your sale is closed through an escrow agent, the agent will usually have their own form of escrow agreement which the parties must execute. If your buyer is paying a portion of the purchase price in a promissory note payable to the seller, a promissory note and security agreement (granting a lien on the business assets) will be delivered to you.

Even if the buyer's attorney drafts the purchase agreement, you will become the "creditor" after the sale, and your attorney should draft the note and security agreement. Escrow agents may offer forms of promissory notes and security agreements as a free service, and these forms are usually worth every penny you pay for them. Do not skimp on the cost of preparing key documents.

The Closing Day

Once all the final documents have been signed, the consent to assignment of the seller's existing contracts have been obtained and any final tax clearance certificates are in hand, the deal can close. The closing day may flow smoothly, with an exchange of signed documents and certificates, delivery of the purchase price for the bill of sale or stock certificates. A business sale has many moving parts, so expect one or two of those parts to fall off the wagon. Keep your cool, trust your attorney and M&A advisor and get the closing payment in hand.

Then, enjoy a closing celebration over dinner. Once the buyer is relatively comfortable in command of the company, take a well-deserved vacation.

Zack, Southern Electrical Supplies

Ella called all the contractual counterparties from whom written consent was required in order to assign such contracts to RCK and close the sale. The most important consent was the assignment of SES's warehouse and office lease. After SES's landlord reviewed RCK's financials, it readily consented to the assignment without personal guaranties, charging a fee of $500 for its assignment. Each remaining consent was obtained, or notifications delivered well before closing.

Since SES earned its revenue selling inventory from stock, it was obligated to comply with Bulk Sales Laws, open an escrow and send notices to all its creditors. Its creditors, including its bank and various vendors, submitted claims for payment to the escrow agent, and all such creditors were paid from escrow at closing. All state taxes related to the sale were also paid by escrow. The escrow agent obtained tax clearance certificates.

Ella and SES's associate attorney updated SES's disclosure schedules as required under the asset purchase agreement. RCK, SES and Zack executed all the agreements and delivered them to the escrow agent to hold in trust until closing, including the non-compete and consulting agreements.

On the closing date all of SES's employees were terminated and received their final paychecks from SES, then immediately rehired by RCK.

On the closing date, RCK wired to escrow the sum of $15,512,500 ($15.5 million, plus half of the escrow's $25,000 fee). Creditors, including SES's bank, were paid roughly $426,000 from the closing proceed. SES's M&A advisor was paid a fee of $255,000 calculated on the net price paid at closing. SES's proceeds were divided among its multiple entities. Zack used corporate funds to pay his outstanding attorney's fees of $27,500 and CPA fees of $7,500.

The phantom stockholders received a total of $1,741,980. Their loyalty to SES helped build the business and attract the price paid by RCK. The remaining $12.8 million was paid into the SES corporations, used to pay pension fund contributions, health and life insurance premiums, and large distributions to Zack which he invested into a mix of investments chosen by his wealth advisor.

Two of SES's corporations were kept active for several years to pay any ongoing costs and address any contingent liabilities.

Zack provided consulting services to RCK at a diminishing rate over the 12 months after closing. He was able to attend his children's sporting events and take his family on multiple vacations over the next 10 years. He finally moved out of the house he remodeled during his AVX years and into a home that was big enough to entice two of his children to move back home after college.

Harry, Elegant Catering

Fortunately, Indulge was nearing the end of its lease in Dana Point and would move its kitchen into the space Elegant Catering leased in 2016. Elegant Catering's landlord reviewed the tax returns and credit reports of Indulge and their owners. The landlord granted consent to Elegant Catering's assignment of the lease, charging a fee of $750. All the new owners were required to guaranty the lease, but Dr. Brennan refused. Elegant Catering's landlord allowed the assignment without Dr. Brennan's guaranty, but he would not release Harry from his personal guaranty.

The buyers' attorney drafted a non-compete agreement which barred Harry from any participation in the catering business in Orange County for five years. Harry readily accepted the non-compete.

The buyers interviewed Elegant Catering's employees and decided to keep all of them employed except for the three who recently quit Indulge to join Elegant Catering. Finally, with Harry's permission the buyers met with the managers of Bayside View and the other properties where Elegant Catering provided their services. Although the properties seemed concerned that this concentration would cause upward pricing pressure, the management of each property were pleased to be working with the more reliable and professional management of Indulge.

On the closing date, Elegant Catering formally terminated all its employees and issued their final paychecks with all accrued vacation. Harry paid his employment attorney $900 for her advice on properly terminating and paying Elegant Catering's employees. Harry was anxious about these employment issues.

The closing was delayed until May 15, 2020, and upon execution and delivery of a bill of sale and other closing documents, escrow released to Elegant Catering $453,500, equal to the $700,000 fixed price, less the 10% broker's fee, half of the escrow fees of $5,000, and less the $174,000 balance owed to the IRS and EDD.

Harry mailed a $20,000 check to Nilufer and called to ask if he could return to New York. Nil was away in Seoul, Korea for six months restructuring the debt of a Korean chaebol. She promised to stay in touch via email and call him again when she returned to New York.

Three weeks after the closing, the new owners told Harry he did not have to return to work again. Harry took a two-week vacation to Cabo San Lucas.

A week after returning from his vacation, Harry called his CPA at Farley & Co. He asked his CPA if he could do anything to reduce the taxable gain he would recognize in 2020. His CPA asked if the parties had agreed upon the purchase price allocation, but, unfortunately, this remained an open item to be agreed upon post-closing. His CPA explained that the ship had sailed on many alternatives to mitigate or defer the taxable gain. However, his CPA offered to analyze the alternatives of rolling over the proceeds from the sale into a qualified opportunity fund.

After the closing, the cash from the sale remained parked in bank accounts of Elegant Catering and Harry, less the sums he spent on vacation, repaid to Nil and used to pay off credit cards. Harry planned to rely on Nil's Wall Street expertise when investing his new wealth. Nil emailed Harry to explain that she was not a wealth advisor and would be uncomfortable advising him how to invest this much money.

Frustrated, Harry called a financial advisor who previously worked with Harry as a mortgage broker. This advisor quickly prepared agreements to manage Harry's liquid accounts. Within two days Harry owned accounts holding $415,000 of Exchange Traded Funds. The mix of funds remained largely unchanged for the next six years, yielding returns ranging from six percent to eight percent per year, less a fee of one percent charged by Harry's advisor.

Harry withdrew $285,000 of these funds over the three years after closing the sale. After a year of considering career options, Harry went back to work as a mortgage broker in Dana Point.

Exhibit A

RECIPROCAL CONFIDENTIALITY AND NONDISCLOSURE AGREEMENT

This Agreement effective as of January 1, 2022 is by and between SELLING BUSINESS, INC. a Delaware corporation ("Seller") on the one hand, and Emma Wealthy, an individual and NEWCO, LLC, a Delaware limited liability company (collectively, "Buyer") on the other hand. The parties intend to exchange or have exchanged Confidential Information as a part of their discussions regarding possible or current ongoing business "Transaction(s)" between them. The parties hereto agree to be bound by all of the following terms and conditions:

1. DEFINITIONS

1.1. "Discloser" means the party disclosing Confidential Information to Recipient for evaluation by the employees, officers and directors, affiliates, agents, professional advisors, consultants and independent contractors of Recipient.

1.2. "Recipient" means the party receiving Confidential Information and includes the employees, officers and directors, affiliates, agents, professional advisors, consultants and independent contractors of Recipient.

1.3. "Confidential Information" means all information and material which is proprietary to Discloser which may be marked or otherwise identified as "confidential" or "proprietary" and which otherwise is disclosed to or obtained by Recipient, pursuant hereto. Confidential information includes, but is not limited to past, present and planned business activities, designs, drawings, specifications, techniques, models, data, source code, object code, documentation, diagrams, flow charts, research, development, processes, procedures, "know-how", new product or new technology information, formulae, product prototypes, product copies, manufacturing, development or marketing techniques and materials, development or marketing timetables, strategies and development plans, including trade names, trademarks, customer, consultant, supplier or employee and personnel names and identities and other information related to customers, suppliers, employees, consultants, or personnel, pricing policies and financial information, and other information of a similar nature, whether or not reduced to writing or other tangible form, and any other trade secrets or nonpublic business information. Confidential Information also includes the existence of this Agreement between the parties and fact they have engaged in discussions relating to a possible business transaction between them. Confidential Information does not include any information which: (a) was in the lawful and unrestricted possession of Recipient prior to its disclosure by Discloser; (b) is or becomes generally available to the public by acts other than those of Recipient after receiving it; (c) has been received lawfully and in good faith by Recipient from a third party who did not derive it from Discloser; or (d) is shown by acceptable evidence have been independently developed by the Recipient.

2.   OBLIGATIONS

2.1.   Recipient will hold in complete confidence and not disclose, produce, publish, permit access to, or reveal the Confidential Information, at any time, without the express prior written consent of Discloser. Recipient agrees to use at least the same degree of care, but no less than a reasonable degree of care, to avoid unauthorized disclosure or use of the Confidential Information as Recipient employs with respect to its own proprietary information of like importance.

2.2.   Recipient will not copy, photograph, photocopy, alter, modify, disassemble, reverse engineer, decompile, or in any manner reproduce any materials containing or constituting Confidential Information unless as required or in connection with the current or contemplated business relationship between the Parties or as part of regularly scheduled automatic backups of all data files on the Recipient's computers and/or servers. Recipient will return all such tangible materials, together with any copies thereof to the fullest extent practicable, promptly after the purposes for which they were furnished have been accomplished, or upon the request of Discloser. Upon request of Discloser, Recipient will destroy all tangible materials, including notes, summaries, memoranda, drawings, manuals, records, excerpts or derivative information, received or prepared by Recipient that contain Confidential Information. Recipient will take all available and reasonable measures to destroy all automatic backup copies of Confidential Information, including electronic copies stored offsite, to the extent practicable.

2.3. Recipient will not publish any review, notice or other report concerning any Confidential Information. Reviews, notices or other reports concerning Confidential Information which are not authorized by Discloser will not release Recipient from any of its obligations hereunder.

2.4. Recipient may disclose Confidential Information in response to a valid order of a court, provided Recipient first gives notice to Discloser and makes a reasonable effort to obtain a protective order requiring that the Confidential Information be disclosed only for limited purposes for which the order was issued.

2.5. Recipient shall use the Confidential Information only for the purpose of evaluating the possible business transaction between the parties or for any other purpose authorized by the Discloser. Recipient shall disclose Confidential Information only to its own employees having a need to know.

2.6. Upon discovery by Recipient of any inadvertent or unauthorized disclosure or use of such Confidential Information, Recipient shall inform Discloser of the specific facts of the inadvertent or unauthorized disclosure or use, and, Recipient shall take all steps reasonably necessary to prevent any further inadvertent or unauthorized disclosure or use of the Confidential Information.

2.7. Upon its execution by both parties, this Agreement shall become effective for a term beginning as of the Effective Date and shall continue to apply to all information exchanged by the Parties for so long as the parties maintain a contractual relationship related to the business transaction(s) described in the initial paragraph of this Agreement, but in no event shall the term of this Agreement be for a period longer than five (5) years from the date of this Agreement. Either party may terminate this Agreement by providing thirty (30) days written notice to the other. Notwithstanding the above, the provisions in this Section 2 concerning the use and protection of Confidential Information received under this Agreement shall survive the termination of this Agreement and remain in effect for a period of three (3) additional years after the expiration or termination of this Agreement.

2.8. Without the prior written consent of the other Party, neither Party will, and such Party will cause its Representatives not to, make any release to the press or other public disclosure, or make any statement to any employee, competitor, customer, client or supplier of the other Party or any of its subsidiaries or any other person, with respect to either the fact that discussions or negotiations are taking place concerning the Transaction or the existence or contents of this Agreement, except for such public disclosure as may be necessary for the Party proposing to make the disclosure not to be in violation of or default under any applicable law, regulation or governmental order.

3.   SOLICITATION.   Each party agrees that it will not solicit employees or consultants of the other party and will not, directly or indirectly, either for itself or any other person, (a) induce or attempt to induce any employee of the other party to leave the employ of such party, (b) in any way interfere with the relationship between the other party and any consultant, personnel or employee of the other party, (c) employ, or otherwise engage as an employee, independent contractor, or otherwise, any employee or consultant of the other party, or (d) induce or attempt to induce any customer, supplier, consultant, licensee, or business relation of the other party to cease doing business with the other party, or in any way interfere with the relationship between any customer, supplier, consultant, employee, personnel, licensee, or business relation of the other party.

4. <u>RESERVATION OF RIGHTS.</u> Confidential Information disclosed to Recipient shall remain the property of Discloser.

4.1. <u>NO IMPLIED LICENSE.</u> No rights or obligations other than those expressly recited herein are to be implied form this Agreement. No license is hereby granted, directly or indirectly, to any of the information disclosed.

5. <u>INJUNCTIVE RELIEF.</u> Each Party agrees that (i) money damages are not a sufficient remedy for any breach of any provision of this Agreement by the other Party and (ii) any unauthorized use or disclosure of the Information provided to the Receiving Party by the Disclosing Party will cause irreparable harm to the Disclosing Party. In addition to all other remedies which any Party hereto may have, each Party will be entitled to seek specific performance and injunctive or other equitable relief as a remedy for any such breach without the need to post any bond. No failure or delay by any Party hereto in exercising any right, power or privilege hereunder will operate as a waiver thereof, nor will any single or partial exercise thereof preclude any other or further exercise thereof or the exercise of any right, power or privilege hereunder. All injunctive remedies are in addition to all other legal remedies the Parties may pursue.

6. <u>MISCELLANEOUS</u>

6.1. <u>GOVERNING LAW, JURISDICTION AND VENUE.</u> This Agreement will be governed by and construed in accordance with the laws of the State of California without reference to its choice of law rules and as if wholly to be performed within the State of California. Any litigation regarding the interpretation, breach or enforcement of this agreement will be filed in and heard only by the state or federal courts with jurisdiction to hear such disputes in Los Angeles County, California, the parties hereby expressly submit to the jurisdiction of such courts.

6.2. <u>ATTORNEYS' FEES.</u> If any judicial or other proceeding is brought by either party regarding the interpretation or enforcement of this Agreement, the prevailing party may recover from the other all costs, attorneys' fees and other expenses incurred by the prevailing party with regard to that proceeding. The right to such costs, attorneys' fees and other expenses shall be deemed to have accrued upon the commencement of said proceeding and shall be enforceable whether or not said proceeding is prosecuted to judgment.

6.3. <u>ENTIRE AGREEMENT.</u> This Agreement sets forth the entire understanding and agreement between the parties with respect to the subject matter hereof and supersedes all other oral or written representations and understandings.

6.5 <u>NOTICES.</u> All notices, requests, and demands and other communications hereunder shall be in writing; shall be personally delivered, sent by registered or certified mail, postage prepaid, return receipt requested, or sent by commercially recognized courier service; and shall be deemed delivered upon receipt by the party to whom addressed, as set forth below:

If to Seller: _____

                   _____

                   _____

If to Buyer: _____

                   _____

                   _____

Either party can change its address by giving notice in writing of the changed address to the other party in accordance with the terms of this Section 6.5.

6.6 SUCCESSORS AND ASSIGNS. This Agreement is binding upon successors, assigns and legal representatives of the parties, and protects Confidential Information of any successors or assigns of the parties.

6.7. AUTHORITY. Each of the persons executing this Agreement represents that he/she is authorized to execute on behalf of, and to therefore bind, the entity, if any, indicated below.

6.8 AMENDMENT IN WRITING. Any amendment of this Agreement must be in writing and signed by each Party. It is expressly understood that this Agreement is not intended to, and does not, constitute an agreement to consummate the Transaction(s) or to enter into a definitive agreement related thereto, and neither Party will have any rights or obligations of any kind whatsoever with respect to such Transaction by virtue of this Agreement or any other written or oral expression by its respective Representatives unless and until a definitive agreement between the Parties is executed and delivered, other than for the matters specifically agreed to herein.

IN WITNESS HEREOF, the parties hereby execute this Non-disclosure Agreement as of the date first set forth above.

SELLING BUSINESS, INC.

By: _____
Michael J. Diaz
Its Chief Executive Officer

NEWCO, LLC

By: _____
Emma Wealthy
Its Manager

EMMA WEALTHY

_____

Exhibit B

February 3, 2022

PERSONAL AND CONFIDENTIAL

Dr. George Retirement
Texas Medical Clinic
5333 Rio Grande Rd.
Corpus Christi, TX 78401

Re: Letter of Intent to Purchase Texas Medical Clinic Assets

Dear Dr. Retirement,

We are pleased to present this letter of intent (the "Letter of Intent") that includes the terms and conditions upon which Conglomerate Health Services, Inc., or its designee ("we" or "Buyer"), would be willing to acquire certain assets of George Retirement MD APC doing business as Texas Medical Clinic (collectively, the "Seller") comprising the orthopedic medicine business located at 5333 Rio Grande Rd., Corpus Christi, TX 78401 (the "Practice").

We propose the following:

1.   Purchase Agreement.   During the next sixty (60) days, Buyer and Seller intend to work together to negotiate a definitive purchase agreement and related and collateral documentation (collectively, the "Agreements") consistent with this Letter of Intent.

2.   Terms.   The terms of the Agreements shall include the following:

(a)   We will purchase substantially all of the assets comprising and used in the operations of the Practice, consisting of all furniture, fixtures, office equipment, computer equipment, medical equipment, inventory, other personal property, contract rights, prepaid expenses and deposits, business records and data, medical records we deem necessary to operate the business, goodwill and other intangible assets, and other related assets used in the operation of the Practice (the "Assets"), but excluding, accounts receivable, real property, cash on hand, and other items agreed upon by Buyer and Seller.

(b)   We will pay Seller Three Million Dollars ($3,000,000) for the Assets as follows: (i) Two Million Seven Hundred Thousand Dollars ($2,700,000) paid in immediately available funds at closing, and (ii) Three Hundred Thousand Dollars ($300,000) paid in immediately available funds twelve (12) months after the closing (subject to offset to satisfy Seller's indemnification obligations described below, taking into consideration the Basket (as hereinafter defined)).   In addition to the above upfront cash purchase price, Dr. Retirement will be eligible for a one-time additional cash payment based on the profitability of the Practice. The cash payment shall be equal to total EBITDA for the Practice exceeding $275,000 for the Buyer's 2023 fiscal year times a multiple of 4.0. For example, if EBITDA for the Practice for fiscal 2023 equals $450,000, an additional cash payment will be made to Dr. Retirement totaling $700,000 [$450,000 - $275,000 = $175,000 x 4.0 = $700,000]. The cash payment will be payable within sixty (60) days after the end of fiscal 2023 (subject to offset to satisfy Seller's indemnification obligations described below). In determining EBITDA for the Practice no corporate allocations will be made to the Practice's costs.

(c) In addition to our purchase of the Assets we will assume Seller's real estate lease for the Practice location; provided, however, that (i) we shall be consulted during Seller's lease renewal negotiations with Seller's landlord, and (ii) the terms and conditions of the lease renewal must be similar or superior to the current lease terms and conditions or be otherwise satisfactory to Buyer. Additionally, we will potentially assume certain of Seller's equipment leases and contracts that we believe are necessary for us to effectively operate the Practice. To clarify, as this is an asset purchase, except as to leases and contracts specifically to be assumed in accordance with the Agreements, we will not assume other liabilities, such as unnecessary equipment leases, loans, notes, lines of credit, obligations to affiliates, contract obligations, employee benefit liabilities, payroll taxes, accrued and unpaid payroll obligations, accrued vacation or other paid time off, state and federal income and other taxes, and litigation and other claims.

(d)　As a condition to closing, we will require that Dr. Retirement enter into Buyer's standard physician employment agreement (including termination only upon written notice, non-competition and non-solicitation covenants) for full-time employment with Buyer or an affiliate of Buyer, with base compensation of $325,000 per year plus a $25,000 per year stipend for service as a Center Medical Director, standard benefits and other terms of employment that are mutually acceptable to the parties. The term of the employment agreement will be three (3) years, with annual automatic one-year renewal terms thereafter. In addition to base compensation, the physician will be eligible for a bonus program in-line with other Conglomerate physicians serving the organization in similar capacities.

(e)　As a condition to closing we may require that certain other key individuals enter into standard employment agreements (which may include non-competition and non-solicitation covenants) with Buyer or an affiliate of Buyer. Those individuals will be identified by Buyer during Buyer's due diligence investigation pursuant to Section 4 below. As to other employed individuals, we intend to hire those employees of Seller that we believe are necessary for the continued effective and efficient operation of the Practice. We expect that any employee we hire will retain the employee's seniority date for purposes of benefit eligibility.

(f)　Seller will purchase, at Seller's expense, malpractice "tail" insurance for prior acts coverage for the Practice, Seller, and all past and present physicians and other providers who provide or have provided services at, for, or in connection with the Practice, provided that such insurance coverage is on a "claims-made" basis. Any such "tail" insurance coverage shall be effective for a period of at least four (4) years from the closing date, shall have coverage limits of $1 million per claim or medical incident/$3 million annual aggregate per provider, and shall otherwise be in form and substance satisfactory to Buyer.

(g) The Agreements will include a non-competition covenant restricting Seller and Dr. George Retirement from owning or managing a business in competition with Buyer's clinic activities within twenty (20) miles of the Practice locations for a period of five (5) years from the closing date. In addition, the Agreements will include a covenant restricting Seller and Seller's equity holders' and affiliates' solicitation of any client of the Practice or client of Buyer and its affiliates and any employee of Buyer and its affiliates for a period of five (5) years from the closing date.

(h) The representations and warranties, however, will only survive for a period of three (3) years following the closing date, except for customary fundamental representations and warranties (i.e. organization and good standing, ownership and capitalization and no finder's or broker's fees (the "Fundamental Representations")). Furthermore, except as to indemnification obligations resulting from breaches of Fundamental Representations, the Seller's total indemnification obligation shall not exceed twenty percent (20%) of the purchase price for the Assets set forth in the Agreements, inclusive of both the initial purchase price and any earn out (the "Cap Amount"); provided, however, that the Cap Amount may be reduced upon mutual agreement of the parties based upon risks assessed by Buyer as a result of due diligence, but not below amounts customary for similar transactions. Furthermore, except as to indemnification obligations resulting from breaches of Fundamental Representations, Seller shall not be liable to Buyer for indemnification except for such losses in excess of aggregate losses equal to Fifty Thousand and No/100 Dollars ($50,000.00) (the "Basket").

(i) The Agreements shall contain other provisions, representations, warranties, and covenants by Seller that are customary with respect to transactions such as the transactions contemplated by this Letter of Intent, including, without limitation, customary provisions regarding indemnification of Buyer by Seller, without deductible, for breaches of representations, warranties, and covenants.

3. <u>Conditions Precedent.</u> The execution and delivery of the Agreements and the consummation of the transactions contemplated by this Letter of Intent and the Agreements shall be subject in all respects to the prior satisfaction of the following conditions:

(a) Buyer and its representatives shall have been afforded an opportunity to conduct a due diligence investigation of the Practice, books, records, properties, operations, finances, facilities, and historical and projected results and operations of Seller and the Practice and to interview key personnel of Seller and the Practice, and shall be satisfied with the results;

(b)   The Agreements, and all collateral documentation, shall be in form and substance satisfactory to Buyer and Seller;

(c)   There shall have been no material adverse change in the market, business, financial condition, prospects, management, ownership, or structure of the Practice or the Assets;

(d)   All material representations concerning Seller and the Practice, and their business, properties, operations, and finances given in the course of Buyer's due diligence investigation shall be true, correct, and complete in all respects;

(e)   All regulatory approvals and all licenses necessary for operating the Practice under the ownership of Buyer shall have been obtained; and

(f)   The lease renewal terms and conditions for the Practice's real property lease shall be similar or superior to the terms and conditions of the current lease, or Buyer shall be otherwise satisfied with the terms and conditions of the lease renewal for the Practice.

4.   Due Diligence Investigation. During the term of this Letter of Intent we will work with Seller to perform a customary due diligence investigation with due concern for Seller's operations and obligations to its patients. Our investigation will include, among other matters, interviews with Seller personnel and access by a limited number of our employees, attorneys, accountants, and other representatives to Seller's premises and

facilities and to Seller's books and records, and operating data related to the Practice.

5. <u>Exclusive Negotiations and Conduct of the Practice.</u> In consideration of the substantial time and expense to Buyer in analyzing the business of Seller and the Practice, in conducting its due diligence investigation, and in preparing this Letter of Intent and the Agreements, during the sixty (60) day period commencing on the date of Seller's acceptance of this Letter of Intent, neither Seller nor any of any of its officers, directors, employees, members, managers, agents, shareholders, or affiliates shall, directly or indirectly, without the prior written consent of Buyer, contact, respond to, negotiate with, or initiate or hold discussions with any corporation, partnership, person, or other entity (other than Buyer) regarding (a) the sale or other disposition of all or any portion of the Assets or the Practice, (b) the sale or other disposition of any stock or other equity interests in Seller, (c) the merger or consolidation of Seller with or into any other entity, or (d) the development, management, or other disposition of all or any portion of the Practice. The sixty (60) day period noted above will be automatically extended for an additional twenty (20) days, unless either of the parties provides written notice of its intent to opt out of the extension at least five (5) days prior to the end of the sixty (60) period.

6. <u>Return of Documents and Confidentiality.</u> We acknowledge that during the course of our due diligence investigation and the negotiation and preparation of the Agreements, we will receive and have access to certain of Seller's confidential and

proprietary information. We agree to share this information only with our agents and employees and to inform them of the restrictions contained in this section. In the event that the transactions contemplated by this Letter of Intent do not occur, for any reason, we will return all documents and records regarding Seller and the Practice that we obtained during the course of our due diligence investigation and will use reasonable efforts to cause all such information to be kept confidential.

7. <u>Expenses.</u> Buyer and Seller shall each be responsible for and shall pay their own respective expenses incurred in connection with this Letter of Intent, the due diligence investigation contemplated hereby, the preparation of the Agreements, and the transactions contemplated by this Letter of Intent and the Agreements, including, without limitation, legal and accounting fees and expenses.

8. <u>No Brokers.</u> Each of the parties' covenants, represents, and warrants to the other that it shall indemnify and hold the other harmless from any claim made through such party by any broker or finder.

9. <u>Termination.</u> This Letter of Intent has a term of sixty (60) days, subject to extension as provided herein, commencing on the date hereof, after which it, and the rights and obligations of Buyer and Seller hereunder, shall terminate, except as otherwise expressly set forth in Section 12 below.

10. <u>Public Announcement.</u> No announcement or disclosure of the proposed transactions contemplated by this Letter of Intent, or of any of the other matters set forth in this Letter of Intent, will be made by either of the parties, without the prior written approval of the other party, except as may be required by law.

11. <u>No Assignment.</u> Neither party may assign any of its rights or obligations hereunder to any other person or entity without the prior written consent of the other party.

12. <u>Non-Binding Letter of Intent.</u> This Letter of Intent is intended to be and shall be construed only as a non-binding letter of intent summarizing and evidencing prior discussions between Buyer and Seller. Neither Buyer nor Seller deems this Letter of Intent to be an offer to purchase the Assets or an agreement in respect thereof. The respective rights and obligations of Buyer and Seller remain to be defined in the Agreements, into which this Letter of Intent and all prior discussions shall merge and be superseded. This Letter of Intent does not create a binding contractual obligation, nor does it obligate either party to enter into the Agreements, nor does it obligate either party to negotiate or take any other action, whether or not expressly or impliedly set forth herein. The parties understand and agree that neither of them will be bound until and unless the formal Agreements have been signed covering all of the foregoing matters and such additional considerations as either party deems appropriate. Efforts by either of the parties to complete due diligence, undertake marketing efforts, prepare the Agreements, or

incur any expense shall not be considered as evidence of intent by either of the parties to be bound by this Letter of Intent. Performance by either of the parties before execution of the final Agreements of any of the obligations which may be included in the final Agreements between the parties when and if negotiations are undertaken or completed shall not be considered evidence of intent by either party to be bound by this Letter of Intent. Anything herein to the contrary notwithstanding, however, the respective obligations of Buyer and Seller as set forth in Sections 5, 6, 8, 9, 10, and 12 of this Letter of Intent shall be binding upon Buyer and Seller and shall survive the termination of this Letter of Intent pursuant to Section 9.

If Seller is in agreement with this Letter of Intent, please sign, date, and deliver it to the undersigned no later than 5:00 p.m., Dallas, Texas, time, on **February 15, 2022**, or this proposal to enter into a Letter of Intent shall be deemed to be revoked and of no further force or effect. Once this Letter of Intent is signed, dated, and delivered by Seller, Buyer will inform its attorneys and employees to proceed with the due diligence investigation and preparation of the Agreements.

Very truly yours,
CONGLOMERATE HEALTH SERVICES, INC.

By: _____

Marcus Buyer
Senior Vice President – Strategy & Corp. Development

ACKNOWLEDGED AND AGREED TO THIS
_____ DAY OF _____, 2022:

GEORGE S. RETIREMENT MD APC

By: _____
George Retirement, M.D.
President

Exhibit C

Due Diligence Request List

General Information				
	Request	**Status/ Delivery**	**Notes & Comments**	
1.1	Organizational Chart			
1.2	Articles, Bylaws, Operating Agreement			
1.3	Fictitious Business Names			
1.4	Management Team: Officers, Directors, key employees			
1.5	Minutes & Actions by Written Consent			
1.6	Shareholders/Owners; Options, Warrants or Other Ownership Interests			
1.7	Jurisdictions Where Company Does Business			
1.8	Agreements Among Shareholders/Owners			
1.9	Special Rights of Any Owners			
Management and Employees				
2.1	Compensation of Directors, Officers and Other Key Members of Management			
2.2	Resumes of Directors, Officers and Other Key Members of Management			
2.3	Employee Handbook			
2.4	Schedule of Benefits and Insurance Policies			

EXHIBIT C

2.5	Payroll Register		
2.6	Description of Hiring Training Processes		
2.7	Schedule of Accrued Vacation and Sick Leave		
2.8	Copies of Benefits and Insurance Policies		
2.9	Employment Contracts		
2.10	Records regarding Immigration Status of all Employees		
Products and Services			
3.1	Details regarding Sales, Cost of Sales of each material individual product or service for the past three years		
3.2	Details projecting Sales, Cost of Sales of each material individual product or service for the next three years		
3.3	Explain variance in sales, cost of sales and gross profit for the past three years		
3.4	Identify most profitable products or services		
3.5	Identify barriers limiting growth in sales of most profitable products or services		
3.6	Identify resources needed to grow sales of most profitable products or services		
3.7	Identify intellectual property or technology needed to grow sales of most profitable products or services		
3.8	New products or services needed to diversify profitable product or service lines		
3.9	Current bid or RFP process for material product or service lines		
Competition			
4.1	List Current Competitors		
4.2	List Future Competitors		

EXHIBIT C

4.3	Key Competitive Factors (price, service, technology, etc.)		
4.4	Advantages Company has over Competition		
4.5	Advantages Competition has over Company		
4.6	Research & Development efforts for new Products or Services		
4.7	Resources Company Needs to Obtain Market Share		
4.8	Current Market Trends		
Customer Information			
5.1	Sales by Customer past 3 years		
5.2	All Customers making up 5% or more of annual sales past 3 years		
5.3	Top ten customers past three years		
5.4	Foreign customers		
5.5	Contracts with Customers		
5.6	Discounts Provided to any customer		
5.7	Warranties to Customers		
5.8	Selection and Targeting of Customers		
5.9	Advertising Expenditures for Past 3 years		
5.10	New Sales Initiatives Under Consideration		
5.11	Financing programs offered to Customers		
5.12	Credit Policies		
5.13	Open Sales Backlogs		
5.14	Deposits, Prepaid Fees and Deferred Revenues		
5.15	Customers over 5% of Sales who terminated Company's services.		
5.16	Variance in Gross Profit to material Customers		
5.17	Any major Customers who are in Financial Distress		

EXHIBIT C

Key Vendors and Service Providers			
6.1	Top 10 Vendors and Service Providers past 3 years		
6.2	Contracts with all vendors and Service Providers		
6.3	Purchases on Consignment from Vendors		
6.4	Foreign Vendors		
6.5	Vendors or Service Providers who have refused to do business with Company		
6.6	Discounts or Special Pricing from Vendors or Service Providers		
6.7	Discounts or Special Pricing about to lapse		
6.8	Product or Service Warranties from Vendors		
6.9	Vendors or Service Providers which are affiliates of Company (related parties)		
6.10	Security Agreements with any Vendors or Service Providers (including UCC-1 financing statements)		
6.11	Financing terms from Vendors or Service Providers		
6.12	Backlog of orders made to Vendors or Service Providers		
6.13	Key Vendors or Service Providers in financial distress		
Technology, Software and Hardware			
7.1	Websites, URLs and Hosting		
7.2	Webmaster, Administrator of All Online Resources		
7.3	Disaster Recovery Program for all data & software		
7.4	Keywords and meta tags and processes used for SEO		

Exhibit C

7.5	Software databases, systems owned, developed or licensed by the Company.		
7.6	Licenses for all software used by the Company, license number and expiration date		
7.7	Schedule of all material ongoing or planned software, database or networking projects. Budgets for same.		
7.8	Cloud based software, where is data stored, licenses, usernames and passwords.		
7.9	Software Developed by the Company or related parties. Restrictions on such software.		
7.10	List all hardware used by Company, on-site and off-site.		
7.11	Restrictions on transfer or change of control of software. Conflicts that might arise from Buyer's use of Software.		
Marketing, Branding and Public Relations			
8.1	Marketing, branding plan		
8.2	Resumes and job descriptions of internal or external branding experts, graphic artists, PR employees		
8.3	All brochures, literature and forms used by Company for marketing		
8.4	Websites and domains used for marketing		
8.5	Trademarks & Applications		
8.6	Trademarks used by not owned		
8.7	Disaster plan in event of highly negative news/events		
8.8	Any marketing and PR reports which are prepared on a regular basis		
8.9	All articles, press releases about the Company and its officers		
8.10	Foreign branding by the Company		

EXHIBIT C

Related Parties and Minority Owners			
9.1	Minority Owners and Percentage of Ownership, including individuals and entities		
9.2	Related parties (officers, directors, shareholders)		
9.3	Employees and service providers who are family members		
9.4	Contracts with related parties or minority owners		
9.5	Troubled relationships with any related parties or minority owners		
9.6	Assets owned by the Company which are in the possession of owners or related parties		
9.7	All benefits provided to related parties, minority owners and family members.		
9.8	Transactions between the Company and related parties.		
Insurance			
10.1	Current Insurance Polices (and details regarding same)		
10.2	Claims on all insurance policies		
10.3	Self-insurance		
10.4	Risks which are not adequately addressed by insurance		
10.5	Buy-sell Agreements among owners		
10.6	Key-Man Life Insurance policies		
10.7	Agents for all insurance policies (and contact information)		
10.8	Insurance policies used to guaranty obligations under other agreements.		
10.9	Rejection of coverage under any insurance policies.		

EXHIBIT C

Financial Information			
11.1	Financial Statements for the past three years		
11.2	Financial projections for the next three years		
11.3	Revenue recognition policies		
11.4	Current accounts receivable, allowance for bad debts and recent write-offs.		
11.5	Notes receivable and copies of same.		
11.6	Current accounts payable. Explain balances over 60 past-due		
11.7	Material accrued liabilities.		
11.8	Debt, notes payable and lines of credit and copies of same.		
11.9	Copies of all material leases		
11.10	Contingent liabilities (depending upon outcome of an event such as litigation, regulatory action, etc.)		
11.11	Business plans used for financing.		
11.12	List of all capital expenditures for the past three years and necessary expenditures for future growth.		
Inventory			
12.1	List of current inventory		
12.2	Obsolete inventory		
12.3	Any issues with inventory shrinkage (disappearing inventory		
12.4	Vendors of Company's inventory		
12.5	Discounts Company receives to purchase its inventory		
Intellectual Property and Intangible Assets ("IP")			
13.1	Trademarks (registered or unregistered, common law)		

Exhibit C

13.2	Patents (registered or unregistered, common law)		
13.3	Copyrights		
13.4	Service Marks		
13.5	Third Party IP used by Company		
13.6	Litigation or Claims regarding IP		
13.7	Royalties paid or received for IP		
13.8	Trade Secrets		
13.9	IP in Development		
13.10	Agreements with Employees and Other Service Providers regarding IP		
13.11	Goodwill owned by the Company		
13.12	Schedule of Intangible Assets Owned by the Company		
Contracts and Leases			
14.1	Debt Schedule, including capital leases		
14.2	Copies of all Lease Agreements		
14.3	All agreements with bankers, lenders and lenders		
14.4	Any agreements to factor receivables		
14.5	All guarantees of Company obligations by individuals		
14.6	All bonding agreements or requirements		
14.7	All contracts or obligations to indemnify officers or directors		
14.8	Copies of all UCC financing statements		
14.9	Contracts which limit the Company's ability to compete in any fashion		
14.10	Contracts which limit the any party's ability to compete against the Company in any fashion		
14.11	Franchise agreements		

EXHIBIT C

14.12	Marketing or public relations contracts		
Litigation and Claims			
15.1	Lawsuits to which Company is a party		
15.2	Threatened Litigation		
15.3	Consents, injunctions, decrees or settlement agreements to which Company is bound which require or prohibit future behavior		
15.4	Claims by any government agency		
15.5	Any arbitration		
15.6	List of any significant legal risks which could lead to litigation or regulatory action		
15.7	Criminal charges against Company or management		
15.8	Legal opinions issued by Company counsel or issued to the Company		
Taxes			
16.1	Copies of all Tax Returns for past five years		
16.2	Changes to Company's tax reporting status or tax policies		
16.3	Notices to Company by any federal, state local or foreign tax authority		
16.4	List of all unpaid taxes		
16.5	List of all NOL carryforwards and details of any deferred tax liabilities		
16.6	Name and contact information for all tax preparers since the Company's inception		
16.7	Tax licenses and any tax exemption certificates		
16.8	Copies of audits, revenue agent reports and settlements, including any proposed adjustments		

EXHIBIT C

16.9	Rulings or concessions that have been obtained from any federal, state local or foreign tax authority		
16.10	List of all foreign jurisdictions (i.e., states) in which the Company does business		
Environmental Checklist			
17.1	Environmental Permits		
17.2	Insurance Covering Environmental Risks		
17.3	Agreements, Decrees, Orders, Judgments, etc. regarding Environmental Obligations		
17.4	Actions or Claims by Government or Private Parties		
17.5	Property Owned or Leased by the Company currently and in the past.		
17.6	List of all hazardous materials used by the Company or stored on Company property		
17.7	All documents regarding Environmental Liabilities		
17.8	All Environmental Impact Reports		
17.9	Environmental Attorneys who have represented the Company		

INDEX

END NOTES

1. "Sugarwood," Ozark, Netflix, July 21, 2017, Streaming video.
2. Gardner H. Russell, *The Effective Entrepreneur How to Make Bad Guys Finish Last*, Advantage Publishing, 1999, p. 146.
3. Robert T. Slee, *Private Capital Markets, Valuation, Capitalization and Transfer of Private Business Interests, Second Edition*, John Wiley & Sons, 2011, p. 564-565.
4. Ibid, p. 565.
5. Dan Roth, *Where's the Business Selling "Tsunami"?* IBG Business Blog, 2015.
6. Ibid.
7. Frederick D. Lipmann, *The Complete Guide to Valuing & Selling Your Business*, Prima Publishing, 2019, p. 5.
8. Rick Rickertsen, *Sell Your Business Your Way*, AMACOM, 2006, p. 99.
9. Larry Reinharz, Managing Director, Woodbridge international, 2013.
10. John H. Brown, *Cash Out Move On: Get Top Dollar - And More - Selling Your Business*, Business Enterprise Press, 2008, p. 100.
11. Maria L. Murphy, CPA, *Mastering accounting for business combinations*, The Journal of Accountancy, March 1, 2019.
12. Ibid.

13. Frederick D. Lipman, *The Complete Guide to Valuing & Selling Your Business*, 2019, p. 14.

14. Ibid, p.15.

15. Les Nemethy, *Business Exit Planning*, John Wiley & Sons, 2011, p. 88.

16. Ibid.

17. Frederick D. Lipman, *The Complete Guide to Valuing & Selling Your Business*, Prima Publishing, 2019, p. 16

18. Rick Rickertsen, *Sell Your Business Your Way*, AMACOM, 2006, p. 21.

19. Kirk Michie, Bernstein, April 2019.

20. Frederick D. Lipman, *The Complete Guide to Valuing & Selling Your Business*, Prima Publishing, 2019, p. 10.

21. Ibid, p. 18.

22. John H. Brown, *Cash Out Move On, Get Top Dollar—And More—Selling Your Business*, Business Enterprise Press, 2008, p. 69.

23. Robert T. Slee, *Private Capital Markets, Valuation, Capitalization and Transfer of Private Business Interests, Second*

24. *Edition*, John Wiley & Sons, 2011, p. 563. Martin Staubus, Employee Stock Ownership Plans, May 2019.

25. Les Nemethy, *Business Exit Planning*, John Wiley & Sons, 2011, p. 6-7.

26. John H. Brown, *Cash Out Move On, Get Top Dollar—And More—Selling Your Business*, Business Enterprise Press, 2008, p. 161.

27.. Laura Fagundes, *Virtual Data Rooms: Everything You Need to Know*, securedocs blog December 23, 2016.